WEREWOLVES

Myth, Mystery, and Magick

Katie Boyd

Schiffer Publishing Ltd

4880 Lower Valley Road, Atglen, Pennsylvania 19310

DEDICATION

For all those who feel the passion and hunger of their own inner beasts.

Text and images by author unless otherwise noted
Cover images: The Letter W. Vector Illustration © Andrey Gurov. Blood drops on red Background © Bram Janssens.

Schiffer Books are available at special discounts for bulk purchases for sales promotions or premiums. Special editions, including personalized covers, corporate imprints, and excerpts can be created in large quantities for special needs. For more information contact the publisher:

Published by Schiffer Publishing Ltd.
4880 Lower Valley Road
Atglen, PA 19310
Phone: (610) 593-1777; Fax: (610) 593-2002
E-mail: Info@schifferbooks.com

For the largest selection of fine reference books on this and related subjects, please visit our website at
www.schifferbooks.com
We are always looking for people to write books on
new and related subjects. If you have an idea for a book
please contact us at the above address.

This book may be purchased from the publisher.
Include $5.00 for shipping.
Please try your bookstore first.
You may write for a free catalog.

In Europe, Schiffer books are distributed by
Bushwood Books
6 Marksbury Ave.
Kew Gardens
Surrey TW9 4JF England
Phone: 44 (0) 20 8392-8585; Fax: 44 (0) 20 8392-9876
E-mail: info@bushwoodbooks.co.uk
Website: www.bushwoodbooks.co.uk

Library of Congress Control Number: 2011929389

Designed by Mark David Bowyer
Type set in Hurry Up / Zurich BT

ISBN: 978-0-7643-3907-3
Printed in the United States of America

TABLE OF CONTENTS

ACKNOWLEDGMENTS

A special thanks to everyone at Schiffer Publishing including Dinah Roseberry and Peter Schiffer. Thank you to all of the amazing comic book printers, writers, and artists for allowing Don Smith and I access to pick your brains, use your illustrations, and summaries to give examples of the evolution of werewolves in comic books.

In addition, a big thank you goes to Don Smith, a wonderful comic book writer with a passion for a good werewolf story and a man with a great heart! Thank you so much for your contributions to this book.

INTRODUCTION

Supernatural creatures are such a fascinating subject to discuss on any level. Remember, being young and watching *Creature Double Feature*? I used to sit comatose to the outside world every Saturday morning when this television show came on. Everyone in my house knew not to disturb me during that time; movies like the *Creature from the Black Lagoon*, *Cat People,* and *The Incredible Two-Headed Transplant* were amazing. I loved how we were introduced to different types of monsters, including the ever-popular werewolf. On a magical and even scientific level the thought of transmogrification is extremely exciting. I can recall when I first got my hands on an antique occult book (I was around 14 years old and my local library at the time had an old occult, alchemy, and religious section of books hiding in the dark corner of a shelf behind the librarian's desk) which had rituals to shapeshift, curses, and so on. So, being very curious, I started reciting age-old words trying to turn my brother into a crow. I don't believe I pronounced one word correctly as it was all in Latin. Unfortunately, I won't be able to find out either as the library no longer holds those books. They say hindsight is 20/20 and it's so true. I'm thankful now that I didn't know Latin back then, as I realize that many of the old occult books never had a banishing or "undo" for their spells...and although my brother was annoying, if the ritual had worked, I would not have wanted him to stay a crow forever. That would have meant explaining things to Mom and Dad (imagine that conversation), then getting grounded for a *very* long time.

Now we all know since the movie *Twilight* first came out that the popularity of vampires and werewolves has exploded. For me though, I have always loved the classic works of Stephen King. Books such as *Silver Bullet* and *Salem's Lot* brought a completely different dynamic to the werewolf topic; it is the opposite of all things *Twilight* where the lines between good and evil do not blur. *Silver Bullet* will always have a little place in my heart; it is a David and Goliath story with a good amount of humor thrown in. Nevertheless, *Salem's Lot* in its intensity was a fantastic masterpiece of King's fictional horror. I consider movies, books, and the internet to be our collective modern mythology. Thanks to the work of Brahm Stoker, Stephanie Meyers, and Anne Rice, vampires have gone from being merciless killers with absolutely no soul to brooding bad boys who glitter like diamonds in the sunlight. That is a part of our modern mythology now. But it also shows the changes and shaping of cultures. With the advent of the Internet our world has gotten much, much smaller and I find that the mythologies which used to have a regional focus are now extremely mixed.

But do such creatures truly exist or is it our own imagination that brings life to an otherwise mythical monster? Could the myths be a result of different diseases or illnesses which through time have been misunderstood? Could there be such curses out there in the world that forces a human's shape to torturously contort into a wolf-like being during the full-moon cycle—making them lose all ability to think and feel, causing them to essentially lose their soul? Shapeshifting is not a new topic; there are stories, legends, spells, mantras, and myths that occur within almost every culture on the planet.

I have to approach the idea with an open mind and consider that perhaps such supernatural creatures could exist—who am I to say otherwise? In my line of work as a demonologist and in the area of occult sciences/ crimes, over the years I have seen some very strange and unusual artifacts, individuals, and entities. I must say that "we" as humans have yet to prove with real solid evidence that werewolves truly exist, but perhaps these creatures are right in front of us. One just never knows. My whole idea of writing this book was to lay all the cards on the table, to give all sides, all facts, all myths, and allow the reader to decide for themselves.

For those who have read my works before, I love to include the medical side of life, too. In this book, the reader will learn about medical conditions that may have explained the werewolf phenomena such as Hypertrichosis, Clinical Lycanthropy, Hirsutism, and Rabies—to find out if our ancestors perhaps just over reacted due to the lack of medical knowledge. I will introduce you to different cultural myths and legends, which surround the werewolf. Together we will discover the world of transformation, magick, and techniques that once were believed to turn the practitioner or victim into such creatures as the werewolf.

Join my friend and comic book writer Don Smith as he brings you on a fantastic journey through the transformation of the werewolf in the graphic novel industry. With interviews from heavy hitters and independent writers and artists, his writing will captivate your interest and imagination. Brace yourself, as I will go deep into the darkest minds of those who claim to be flesh eaters, who maul their victims to death.

THERIANTHROPY AND LYCANTHROPY EXPLAINED

What is Therianthropy? It's easiest to start with the etymology of the word *therian* means "beast" in Greek with *anthropos* meaning "man" in the same language. Dictionaries give it two definitions; the first being the ability for a man to shift in and out of an animal form, the second describing that of a deity or mythical creature who is comprised of part animal, and part humanoid appearance. Good examples of these would be Anubis, Horus, the centaur, or satyr.

In our particular case we must look more at the first definition of therianthropy, beneath this umbrella term which covers all animals, not one in particular, and comes with terms such as lycanthropy (werewolf), cyanthropy (were-dog) and ailuranthropy (were-cat). But don't think those are the only animals people have changed into. There are many different beasts including horses, birds, snakes, even ...skunks!

Within our society, therianthropy and all of its branches runs deep within the mythologies, and folklore. However, over time the meaning of both therianthropy and lycanthropy has changed in our society as will be evident later in the book.

1763 engraving depicting a were-tiger by Ian Woodard.

PART ONE

MYTHS

"He himself ran in terror, and reaching the silent fields howled aloud, frustrated of speech. Foaming at the mouth, and greedy as ever for killing, he turned against the sheep, still delighting in blood. His clothes became bristling hair, his arms became legs. He was a wolf, but kept some vestige of his former shape."

~Roman poet Ovid (43 BC – 17 AD)

WERE-BEASTS AROUND THE WORLD

Where the wolves roam so too do the man-wolf legends. During the research process for this book I have found three things to be true. Firstly, every culture has shapeshifting legends; secondly, if there are no wolves in an area, there are were-*something* (such as the were-hyena in Ethiopia); and thirdly, magic, murder, and mayhem follow these creatures wherever they go. For the reasons stated above, I am entitling the following chapters as Were-People as not every one of them have lupine connections, you will encounter were-rats, were-cats, were-crocs and more!

There are over twenty major religions throughout the world and the shapeshifting therianthrope has snuck its way into most of their texts and mythologies, either in the form of God, petitioner, or villain.

In Were-Beasts Around the World, we will travel the globe looking at religious texts, mythologies, and stories to discover where these shapeshifters are hiding!

HINDU

RAKSHA

Hinduism is ranked as the fourth largest religion in the world with over 900 million devotees. Practitioners believe that the Raksha-like people can be either bad or good.

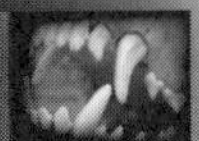

According to the epics and other Hindu lore, Rakshas can live anywhere but they have a tendency to be cannibalistic in nature and love to feast upon the dead flesh after a battle. The Raksha of Hindu mythology is mentioned several times throughout the Hindu holy book the Rig Veda.

RIG VEDA 7.104.22

Destroy the Rakshas who attack like an owl, hound, wolf, eagle, or vulture.

RIG VEDA 7.104.24

O warrior! You should destroy both the male Rakshas and female Rakshas who kills by deceit. May such Rakshas not see the light of dawn.

They are termed as Yatudhaan (those who attack human dwellings) and Kravyaad (those who eat raw flesh).

Within the various Sanskrit epics, we see how the Raksha can be either good or bad. In 1870, Ralph Griffith published a translation of The Ramayan of Valmiki; this text has since become public domain. Canto XIV is the story Rávan Doomed. It clearly indicates the duality of these shapeshifters, Rávan being all that encompasses evil and his brother Vibhishana being a hero who wants nothing more than to be pious and faithful. Cast as the villain Ravana gains so much power that the Gods fear him and pray for a way to end this terror.

RÁVANA

And now with undiminished care
A second rite would fain prepare.
But, O ye Gods, consent to grant
The longing of your supplicant.

For him beseeching hands I lift,
And pray you all to grant the gift,
That four fair sons of high renown
The offerings of the king may crown.
They to the hermit's son replied:
"His longing shall be gratified.
For, Bráhman, in most high degree
We love the king and honour thee."
These words the Gods in answer said,
And vanished thence by Indra led.
Thus to the Lord, the worlds who made,
The Immortals all assembled prayed:
'O Brahmá, mighty by thy grace,
Rávan, who rules the giant race,
Torments us in his senseless pride,
And penance-loving saints beside.
For thou well pleased in days of old
Gavest the boon that makes him bold,
That God nor demon e'er should kill
His charmed life, for so thy will.
We, honouring that high behest,
Bear all his rage though sore distressed.
That lord of giants fierce and fell
Scourges the earth and heaven and hell.
Mad with thy boon, his impious rage
Smites saint and bard and God and sage.
The sun himself withholds his glow.
The wind in fear forbears to blow;
The fire restrains his wonted heat
Where stand the dreaded Rávan's feet,
And, necklaced with the wandering ware,
The sea before him fears to rave.
Kuvera's self in sad defeat
Is driven from his blissful seat.
We see, we feel the giant's might.

And woe comes o'er us and affright.
To thee, O Lord, thy suppliants pray
To find some cure this plague to stay.

Listening to the words of the immortals, Brahma knew he had to find a solution. Rávan was getting out of hand, and although Brahma had promised this villain that no god, demon, nor spirit of air or earth would harm him, Brahma was set to the task of finding a loophole. Suddenly it came to him; he had promised Rávan that none of these powerful beings could cause the evil one harm. But Rávan had neglected to ask the same of the humans! There was a way! Lord Vishnu came in as God of Gods and the other laid their ideas before him, that he should separate himself into three, and become the children of King Da'sarantha's three wives.

The Gods replied: "We fear, O Lord,
Fierce Rávan, ravener abhorred.
Be thine the glorious task, we pray,
In human form this fiend to slay.
By thee of all the Blest alone
This sinner may be overthrown.
He gained by penance long and dire
The favour of the mighty Sire.
Then He who every gift bestows
Guarded the fiend from heavenly foes,
And gave a pledge his life that kept
From all things living, man except.
On him thus armed no other foe
Than man may deal the deadly blow.
Assume, O King, a mortal birth,
And strike the demon to the earth."
Then Vishnu, God of Gods, the Lord
Supreme by all the worlds adored,

To Brahmá and the suppliants spake:
"Dismiss your fear: for your dear sake
In battle will I smite him dead,
The cruel fiend, the Immortal's dread,
And lords and ministers and all
His kith and kin with him shall fall.
Then, in the world of mortal men,
Ten thousand years and hundreds ten
I as a human king will reign,
And guard the earth as my domain."

Within Vishnu down on earth The All God went on to get each of the gods to head down there as well, as shapeshifters:

When Vishnu thus had gone on earth.
From the great king to take his birth.
The self-existent Lord of all
Addressed the Gods who heard his call:
"For Vishnu's sake, the strong and true.
Who seeks the good of all of you,
Make helps, in war to lend him aid,
In forms that change at will, arrayed,
Of wizard skill and hero might,
Outstrippers of the wind in flight,
Skilled in the arts of counsel, wise,
And Vishnu's peers in bold emprise;
With heavenly arts and prudence fraught,
By no devices to be caught;
Skilled in all weapon's lore and use
As they who drink the immortal juice.
And let the nymphs supreme in grace,
And maidens of the minstrel race,

Monkeys and snakes, and those who rove
Free spirits of the hill and grove,
And wandering Daughters of the Air,
In monkey form brave children bear.
So erst the lord of bears I shaped,
Born from my mouth as wide I gaped."
Thus by the mighty Sire addressed
They all obeyed his high behest,
And thus begot in countless swarms
Brave sons disguised in sylvan forms.
Each God, each sage became a sire,
Each minstrel of the heavenly quire,
Each faun, of children strong and good
Whose feet should roam the hill and wood.
Snakes, bards, and spirits, serpents bold
Had sons too numerous to be told.
Báli, the woodland hosts who led,
High as Mahendra's lofty head,
Was Indra's child. That noblest fire,
The Sun, was great Sugríva's sire,
Tára, the mighty monkey, he
Was offspring of Vrihaspati:
Tára the matchless chieftain, boast
For wisdom of the Vánar host.
Of Gandhamádan brave and bold
The father was the Lord of Gold.
Nala the mighty, dear to fame,
Of skilful Vis'vakarmá came.
From Agni, Nila bright as flame,
Who in his splendour, might, and worth,
Surpassed the sire who gave him birth.

As you can see, within Hindu mythology shapeshifting was a fairly common practice. In the end of the epic, Rávan was killed:

He turned the point at Lanká's lord,
And swift the limb-dividing dart
Pierced the huge chest and cleft the heart,
And dead he fell upon the plain
Like Vritra by the Thunderer slain.
The Rákahas host when Rávan fell
Sent forth a wild terrific yell,
Then turned and fled, all hope resigned,
Through Lanká's gates, nor looked behind
His voice each joyous Vánar raised,
And Ráma, conquering Ráma, praised.
Soft from celestial minstrels came
The sound of music and acclaim.
Soft, fresh, and cool, a rising breeze
Brought odours from the heavenly trees,
And ravishing the sight and smell
A wondrous rain of blossoms fell:
And voices breathed round Raghu's son:
"Champion of Gods, well done, well done."

As I said, not all shapeshifters are negative. They fall into categories, such as the Yakshas, which are more like those of Rávan's nature; they are similar to Titans or enemies of the Gods. Then you have the more commonly recognized ones, which are like fiends or demons. There are a wide range of these types of entities. They are shapeshifters by nature. However, their natural shapes vary between beautiful and hideous. Usually larger than the average human, they have some sort of basic animalistic quality to them, but they are typically of a humanoid look. Rávan himself had ten heads in the mythology, while his

brother was absolutely gorgeous. They are the extremes of opposition in example of Raksha.

NORSE

WOLF GOD & DOOMSDAY PROPHECY

In Norse mythology, Loki and his brother, Odin, were destined to be enemies. This makes sense as Odin is about order and Loki is about tricks and chaos. Like a scene from *Star Wars,* Loki is hearkened over to the "darkside" and betrays his brother. Afterwards, Loki goes into exile in Jutenheim, the land of the giants. Over time, Loki ends up siring three children with the giantess known as Angrboda (her name means "the distress bringer"); his three offspring were Fenrir, Hel, and Jörmungandr.

You can think of these three siblings much in the same way as the four horsemen, they bring with them destruction, chaos, and the end of the world. Hel, the only daughter of Loki, appears as a hag—her head and torso is that of a living human but her lower half is that of a corpse. Being the youngest of the trio, she is the keeper of Niflheim, the realm of the dead who have not died in battle.

Fenrir and Odin by Lorenz FrØlich.

Odin and Fenriswolf Freyr and Surt by Emil Draper 1905.

The Binding of Fenrir by George Wright.

She keeps on her person a knife called "Famine," a plate called "Hunger," and a bed called "Disease." Jörmungandr, the middle child, is also known as the Serpent of Midgard. It is said that at the Ragnarok (the final battle), he will defeat Thor.

But where we want to focus is on the eldest of the three, Fenrir, a Wolf-God bred for destruction and mayhem, he is also believed to be the one to begin the end of the world and that he would defeat Odin at Ragnarok.

In the story, "The Binding of Fenrir," when Odin and the others learned about the birth of Loki's children, a prophecy was told that these offspring would threaten the world of man and the gods. When they discover the location of Fenrir, Hel, and Jörmungandr, the All-Father Odin sends some of the gods on a mission to capture the children of his enemy saying:

> Much evil will come upon us, O my children, from this giant brood if we defend not ourselves against them. For their mother will teach them wickedness and still more quickly will they learn the cunning wiles of their father. Fetch me them here, therefore, that I may deal with them forthwith.

When the three were set before Odin at his seat of judgment, he looked at the sad Hel and said to her, "Thou art the bringer of Pain to man and Asgard is no place for such as thou. But I will make thee ruler of the Mist Home, and there shalt thou rule over that unlighted world, the Region of the Dead."

He then flung Jörmungandr into the ocean as he was the bringer of sins and evil thinking. The serpent grew so quickly that within a day he encircled the earth and bit his tail. At times, this son of a god got so upset over his exile he would thrash about causing the tidal waves and rough waters.

Odin finally came to the eldest of the trio, the wolf Fenrir, who was so ugly a monster that none could bear to look upon him. Odin decided to keep him in Aesgard and raise him, only Tyr, God and warrior, was brave enough to feed Fenrir. The wolf-monster continued to grow and grow, and as he grew, so did his ferocity Odin knew he was running out of time and that no matter what nurturing was bestowed upon him, Fenrir could not deny his nature. Odin also knew that he could not kill Fenrir and taint his sacred home with the blood of a wolf, so they decided to bind him.

They created a plan to set before Fenrir a challenge of strength in which he must break the bindings—it was all to be in good fun, or so Fenrir thought. Odin commissioned the other gods to create the chains that the wolf would wear. The first one was titled Leyding, with one kick of his leg Fenrir broke it, the next was called Dromi and Fenrir broke it with a violent shake of his gigantic body. The gods began to lose hope that they would ever be able to bind Fenrir. Odin asked them to make one last ditch effort, he called upon the dwarves and asked them to form a chain of great magic and strength.

> This was made from six things: the noise a cat makes when it moves, the beard of a woman, the roots of a mountain, the sinews of a bear, the breath of a fish, and the spittle of a bird. Since you will have observed that a woman has no beard, a cat makes no noise when running, a mountain has no roots and, upon my word, everything I have told you is just as true, although there are some things that you can't put to the test.

The gods took the rope, then went back to Fenrir. They explained to the wolf that the binding was stronger than it looked which was about the size of a silk cord. Each of the gods tested it and showed that the binding would not

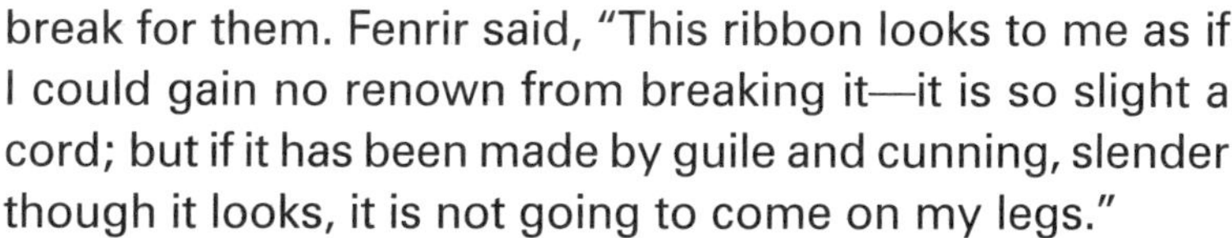

break for them. Fenrir said, "This ribbon looks to me as if I could gain no renown from breaking it—it is so slight a cord; but if it has been made by guile and cunning, slender though it looks, it is not going to come on my legs."

The group assured Fenrir that he would most certainly break this rope as he had done so with the others which were made with much stronger materials. However, if he could not break it they would take it off of him. Fenrir was his father's son and wanted a guarantee that they would release him, so he asked that Tyr, the renowned warrior who specialized in single combat, put his hand into Fenrir's mouth. If they tried to leave him, Tyr would lose the hand that he prized so much. Tyr ended up sacrificing his hand in the binding of Fenrir, the others excited over the fact that they had bound this horrible monster. When they knew for sure that the wolf was truly bound, they fastened a chain called Gegja to it and drew the chain through a giant boulder called Gjöll, which they drove into the earth followed by another huge stone, which they used as a peg. Fenrir outraged opened his gigantic mouth wanting to bite the gods. They shoved a sword into his mouth so that in stood straight up in his lower jaw. He howled in pain and outrage, but the saliva that fell from his mouth produced the river Vón.

The gods thought that was to be the end of their problems with Fenrir, but although bound, the god-son was not done yet. While growing up, Fenrir had visited Midgard (the human realm) and mated with a giantess there, producing two sons Hati and Skoll, both a cross between giant and wolf. Hati chases the chariot that carries the Sun and Skoll chases the one that carries the Moon.

It is prophesied that when it is the time for Ragnarok, these celestial bodies will catch the sun and moon, devouring them. Stars will fall from the sky, trees will die, and Fenris will shake the earth as his bonds break. He will open his mouth so wide that his top jaw will touch the sky and the bottom will hit the earth as he makes ready for the

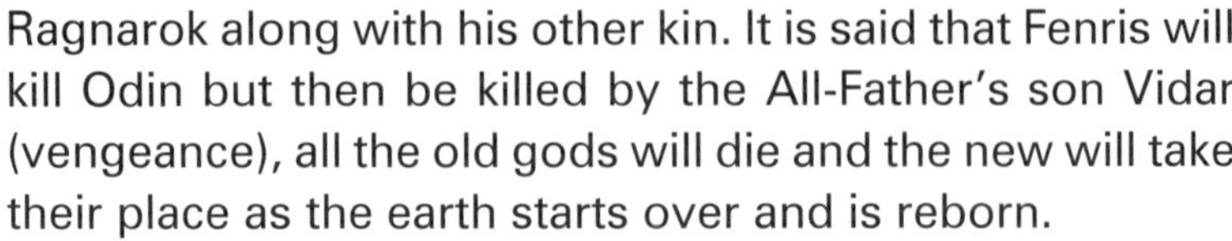

Ragnarok along with his other kin. It is said that Fenris will kill Odin but then be killed by the All-Father's son Vidar (vengeance), all the old gods will die and the new will take their place as the earth starts over and is reborn.

CHRISTIANITY

A WEREWOLF IN THE BIBLE?

BY: DON E. SMITH JR.

> *"Nor did the prophets [doubt]. Did not Daniel warn Nebuchadnezzar? But the proud king did not heed Daniel. And so, as the Bible says, 'He was made as unto a wolf and cast out from men.' A beast has come among us. But God will defend his faithful."*
>
> ~Reverend Fisk
> (*THE WOLFMAN* – 2010)

The Bible is not dull. Some people debate the authenticity of it, some people have used it for the basis of the unspeakable, yet still others believe it to be sacred and, if applied the correct way, it is a book of freedom, understanding, hope, and most of all, love. However, even the most ardent and studious biblical scholar will stray across the oddity even in the Holy Word of God. For example, according to the book of Daniel, the children of Israel had sinned against God. He allowed King Nebuchadnezzar, the king of Babylon, to overthrow Israel. Children and teenagers under the age of 20 were transported to the Babylon (what is today Iraq) and were trained to be part of the Babylonian society. Daniel, along with his friends Shadrach, Meschach, and Abede-engo (from the famous Fiery Furnace story), stuck to their guns and still worshipped the God of Israel. (A relationship with God will pay off for Daniel later in life when he is thrown

into a den of lions). Okay, so what does this have to do with werewolves?

Daniel chapter four has this interesting comment in verse 33:

> The same hour was the thing fulfilled upon Nebuchadnezzar: and he was driven from men, and did eat grass as oxen, and his body was wet with the dew of heaven, till his hairs were grown like eagles' feathers, and his nails like birds' claws.

Or to quote Lehman Strauss, a biblical commentator:

> ...the king became irrational. A form of mental derangement called lycanthropy seized him, a disease whereby a man regards himself to be other than a man. If he thinks himself to be a beast, then to all intents and purposes he behaves like that beast.

So, God inflicted this on Nebuchadnezzar. Why? Let's take this back a little in Daniel chapter twenty-four. Nebuchadnezzar had a dream and Daniel explained it, and let's start with verses 24 through 26.

> This is the interpretation, O king, and this is the decree of the most High, which is come upon my lord the king: That they shall drive thee from men, and thy dwelling shall be with the beasts of the field, and they shall make thee to eat grass as oxen, and they shall wet thee with the dew of heaven, and seven times shall pass over thee, till thou know that the most High ruleth in the kingdom of men, and giveth it to whomsoever he will. And whereas they commanded to leave the stump of the tree roots; thy kingdom shall be sure unto thee, after that thou shalt have known that the heavens do rule.

In verse 27, Daniel warns the king this can be prevented.

> "Wherefore, O king," said Daniel. "Let my counsel be acceptable unto thee, and break off thy sins by righteousness, and thine iniquities by showing mercy to the poor; if it may be a lengthening of thy tranquility."

However, a year later, Nebuchadnezzar is alone, on the roof of his castle. He looks out over his kingdom, he has a swelled head, and in verse 30 he said the following:

> Is not this great Babylon, that I have built for the house of the kingdom by the might of my power, and for the honor of my majesty?

The Almighty was having none of this for while "the word was in the king's mouth, there fell a voice from heaven."

> *"The kingdom is departed from thee,"* said the voice from heaven...

As it said in verse 33,

> The same hour was the thing fulfilled upon Nebuchadnezzar: and he was driven from men, and did eat grass as oxen, and his body was wet with the dew of heaven, till his hairs were grown like eagles' feathers, and his nails like birds' claws.

The famous Biblical commentator Matthew Henry painted the picture this way:

> He is deprived of honor as a man. He loses his reason, and by that means loses his dominion... On a sudden he fell star mad, distracted in the highest degree that every any man was. His understanding and memory were gone, and all the faculties of a rational soul broken, so that he became a perfect brute in the shape of a man.

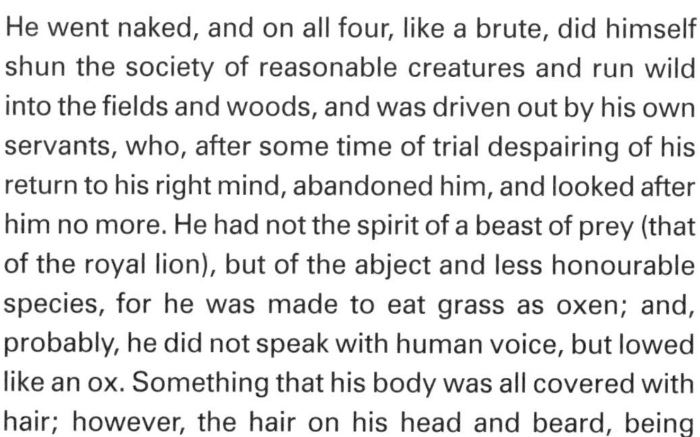

> He went naked, and on all four, like a brute, did himself shun the society of reasonable creatures and run wild into the fields and woods, and was driven out by his own servants, who, after some time of trial despairing of his return to his right mind, abandoned him, and looked after him no more. He had not the spirit of a beast of prey (that of the royal lion), but of the abject and less honourable species, for he was made to eat grass as oxen; and, probably, he did not speak with human voice, but lowed like an ox. Something that his body was all covered with hair; however, the hair on his head and beard, being never cut nor colbed, grew like eagles feathers, and his nails like birds' claws.

"What a monstrosity this man had become!" said another Biblical commentator Oliver Greene.

Why did God choose humble Nebuchadnezzar this way? In the Bible, whenever God humbled anyone, He tended to use a little fire and brimstone, disease, ten plagues, and an invading army. Just ask Israel about that last one. Pastor Fred Provencher of the Cornerstone Christian Church in Wyckoff painted it this way. "God was doing two things here," said Provencher. "He was showing that anyone who walks in pride will be humbled. Second, he was showing that the God of Israel was still above it all."

Provencher explained that with Israel having been conquered by Babylon and repatriated to other parts of the world, it appears as if the God of Israel was beaten badly.

"Nebuchadnezzar's predicament showed Israel, 'I am your God and I am still here'," said Provencher.

Provencher further added, "What is also interesting is that as a beast; he did not harm anyone. He was eating grass."

When it came to running the country for the seven years Nebuchadnezzar was insane, he had his advisors and administrators in place, so that was fine.

"God really was merciful to everyone around Nebuchadnezzar," said Provencher. "He was the only one who was harmed."

However, the upside in this event was after seven years, Nebuchadnezzar repented.

> "...at the end of the days I, Nebuchadnezzar, lifted up mine eyes unto heaven, and mine understanding returned unto me, and I blessed the most High, and I praised and honoured him that liveth for ever, whose dominion is an everlasting dominion, and his kingdom is from generation to generation:"
>
> And all the inhabitants of the earth are reputed as nothing: and he doeth according to his will in the army of heaven, and among the inhabitants of the earth: and none can stay his hand, or say unto him, what doesn't thou?
>
> At the same time my reason returned unto me; and for the glory of my kingdom, mine honour and brightness returned unto me; and my counsellors and my lords sought unto me; and I was established in my kingdom, and excellent majesty was added unto me."
>
> Daniel 4:34 to 36

"It was theologian Tremper Longman who said it best," said Provencher. "'A man who thinks he is like a god must become a beast to learn he is only a human being'."

SHINTO

KITSUNE

The kitsune (which means fox) are servants of Inari Kami, goddess of fertility, rice, all forms of agriculture and, of course, foxes. Throughout many of the Shinto and Buddhist

temples dedicated to Inari, you will find statues of kitsune dressed with a red cloth around their necks.

The Kitsune is believed to possess nine tails, although in most stories they have one, five, or nine (usually not any other number). Some cultures believe the tails only multiply after a kitsune has lived over a thousand years. At that time the fox spirit will actually change color. The kitsune legend spreads further than just the Shinto faith; in Korea, the kitsune is always seen as an evil, sly fox. Korea seems to be one of the only places where the fox spirit is always evil. In Japan and China, they can be either.

If you find yourself in the presence of a malevolent kitsune, be sure to carry some deep fried tofu, as it is one of their favorite treats! They actually have a meal named after them called Kitsune Udon which is an udon noodle soup with deep fried tofu!

A kitsune's natural form is that of a multi-tailed fox but they can shapeshift into almost anything; most commonly they change into humans. It is believed that when you are in the presence of a kitsune that has morphed itself, it will still cast the shadow of a fox. The Kitsune is more than just a shapeshifter, it is believed that it can manifest fire from its tails, enter dreams, create illusions, and cause people to go insane.

GREECE

KING OF THE GODS

KING OF THE WOLVES

Not all werewolves were created by a curse from a parent or an elder, but sometimes from a God. Zeus, King of all kings, King of all Gods and Goddesses, known for being an excellent lover and quite promiscuous did more than just sleep with women. He created a werewolf.

This tale is a cautionary one, if you are having the King of the Gods for dinner, do not feed him a baby.

The reason I speak of Zeus' proclivities is that they do relate to this story. Hera, the King's wife, could not stand his extramarital affairs and changed one of his lovers, Callisto, into that of a bear. Callisto's son, Arcas never knew what became of his mother.

King Lycaon (father of Callisto) had Zeus over for a feast. Upon his plate was the regular meal save for one difference; the meat upon Zeus' plate was that of the child Arcas and served to the god as a meal. But Zeus knew better; upon realizing that the meat he had before him was not that of an animal and had not been properly prepared, the god got angry. So upset was he that he changed King Lycaon into the form of a wolf! Zeus gathered the pieces of Arcas, then reassembled the child (much like what Isis did for Osiris when he was torn to pieces by Set). Eventually, he gave Arcas to Pleaide Maia to be raised as her own.

Later in the mythology, Arcas would grow up and while out hunting, Hera put Callisto before him in her bear form with the intention of Arcas unwittingly killing his mother. Zeus came to the rescue throwing Callisto up into the sky where she formed Ursa Major. Later, Arcas would join her as Ursa Minor. Hera, had to have the last say though; she went to Poseidon and demanded that he let neither of the bears fall into the sea as other stars do, and so Ursa Major and Minor never go below the horizon.

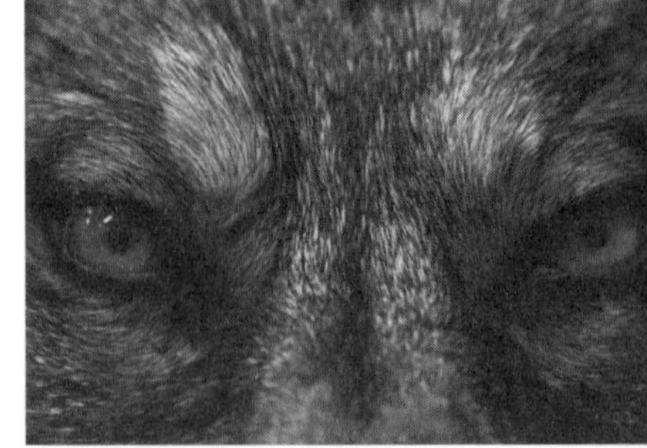

Lycaeon retained his thinking as a man but not his voice; whenever he would attempt to talk to people, he would howl. At least that is one version in Ovid's Metamorphoses: Book 1. He gives in detail what transpired between the two, although in Ovid's version, the god archetype gets a name change to Jupiter:

 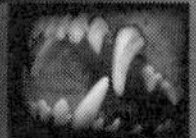

When the noise had subsided, quieted by his royal authority, Jupiter again broke the silence with these words: "Have no fear, he has indeed been punished, but I will tell you his crime, and what the penalty was. News of these evil times had reached my ears. Hoping it false I left Olympus's heights, and travelled the earth, a god in human form. It would take too long to tell what wickedness I found everywhere. Those rumours were even milder than the truth. I had crossed Maenala, those mountains bristling with wild beasts' lairs, Cyllene, and the pinewoods of chill Lycaeus. Then, as the last shadows gave way to night, I entered the inhospitable house of the Arcadian king. I gave them signs that a god had come, and the people began to worship me. At first Lycaon ridiculed their piety, then exclaimed 'I will prove by a straightforward test whether he is a god or a mortal. The truth will not be in doubt.' He planned to destroy me in the depths of sleep, unexpectedly, by night. That is how he resolved to prove the truth. Not satisfied with this he took a hostage sent by the Molossi, opened his throat with a knife, and made some of the still warm limbs tender in seething water, roasting others in the fire. No sooner were these placed on the table than I brought the roof down on the household gods, with my avenging flames, those gods worthy of such a master. He himself ran in terror, and reaching the silent fields howled aloud, frustrated of speech. Foaming at the mouth, and greedy as ever for killing, he turned against the sheep, still delighting in blood. His clothes became bristling hair, his arms became legs. He was a wolf, but kept some vestige of his former shape. There were the same grey hairs, the same violent face, the same glittering eyes, the same savage image. One house has fallen, but others deserve to also. Wherever the earth extends the avenging furies rule. You would think men were sworn to crime! Let them all pay the penalty they deserve, and quickly. That is my intent."

Due to Lycaon's actions and those who Jupiter observed while in human form, he decided it was time to end the race of humans that he loved so dearly. The other gods were with him at first and then they began to think, who would light incense for them? Who would worship at their altars? Jupiter promised to them a better man than his first attempt allowed. He proceeds to devastate the earth with the Deucalian flood. However, that is the Roman version. Here is another variation of the original Greek myth told by Pausanias in his Description of Greece:

> Lykaon the son of Pelasgos devised the following plans, which were more clever than those of his father. He founded the city Lykosoura on Mount Lykaios, gave to Zeus the surname Lykaios and founded the Lykaian games. I hold that the Panathenian festival was not founded before the Lykaian. The early name for the former festival was the Athenian, which was changed to the Panathenian in the time of Theseus, because it was then established by the whole Athenian people gathered together in a single city... My view is that Lykaon was contemporary with Kekrops, the king of Athens, but that they were not equally wise in matters of religion. For Kekrops was the first to name Zeus Hypatos (the Supreme god), and refused to sacrifice anything that had life in it, but burnt instead on the altar the national cakes which the Athenians still call *pelanoi*. But Lykaon brought a human baby to the altar of Zeus Lykaios, and sacrificed it, pouring out its blood upon the altar, and according to the legend immediately after the sacrifice he was changed from a man to a wolf. I for my part believe this story; it has been a legend among the Arkadians from of old, and it has the additional merit of probability. For the men of those days, because of their righteousness and piety, were guests of the gods, eating at the same board; the good were openly honored by the gods, and sinners were openly visited

with their wrath... So one might believe that Lykaon was turned into a beast ...

In Arcadia lies Mt. Lycaeus and it was the home of those who worshipped Wolf-Zeus. Every year they would make a sacrifice to him of meats including a few bits of human flesh. Pausanias goes on to describe the legend as he heard it:

It is said, for instance, that ever since the time of Lykaon a man has changed into a wolf at the sacrifice to Zeus Lykaios, but that the change is not for life; if, when he is a wolf, he abstains from human flesh, after nine years he becomes a man again, but if he tastes human flesh he remains a beast for ever...

Zeus' myth is not the first time that these changes are talked about in the *Satyricon* by Petronius (61 A.D.) which is believed to be one of the first mentions of werewolves. The character describes an event he saw where a man changed his shape into that of a wolf.

Thus when he spake ... he began this tale:

"While I was yet a servant we liv'd in a narrow lane, now the house of Gavilla: There, as the gods would have it, I fell in love with Tarentius's wife; he kept an eating-house. Ye all knew Melissa Tarentina, a pretty little punching-block, and withal beautiful; but (so help me Hercules) I minded her not so much for the matter of the point of that, as that she was good-humour'd; if I asked her anything, she never deny'd me; and what money I had, I trusted her with it; nor did she ever fail me when I'd occasion. It so happened, that a she-companion of hers had dy'd in the country, and she was gone thither; how to come at her I could not tell; but a friend is seen at a dead lift; it also happened my master was gone to Capua to dispatch somewhat or other: I laid hold of the opportunity, and persuaded mine host to take an evenings walk of four or five miles out of town, for he was a stout fellow, and as bold as a devil: The moon shone as bright as day, and about cock-crowing we fell in with a burying-place, and certain monument of the dead: my man loitered behind me a-star-gazing, and I sitting expecting him, fell a singing and numbering them; when looking round me, what should I see but mine host stript stark-naked, and his cloaths lying by the high-wayside.

The sight struck me everywhere, and I stood as if I had been dead; but he piss'd round his cloaths, and of a sudden was turned to a wolf: Don't think I jest; I value no man's estate at that rate, as to tell a lye.

Nevertheless, as I was saying, after he was turned to a wolf, he set up a howl, and fled to the woods. At first I knew not where I was, till going to take up his cloaths, I found them also turn'd to stone. Another man would have dy'd for fear, but I drew my sword, and slaying all the ghosts that came in my way, lighted at last on the place where my mistress was: I entered the first door; my eyes were sunk in my head, the sweat ran off me by more streams than one, and I was just breathing my last, without thought of recovery; when my Melissa coming up to me, began to wonder why I'd be walking so late; and 'if,' said she, 'you had come a little sooner, you might have done us a kindness; for a wolf came into the farm, and has made butchers work enough among the cattle; but tho' he got off, he has no reason to laugh, for a servant of ours ran him through the neck with a pitchfork.' As soon as I heard her, I could not hold open my eyes any longer, and ran home by daylight, like a vintner whose house had been robb'd: But coming by the place where the cloaths were turned to stone, I saw nothing but a puddle of blood; and when I got home, found mine host lying a-bed like an oxe in his stall, and a chirurgeon dressing his neck. I understood afterwards he was a fellow that could change his skin; but from that day forward, could never eat a bit of bread with him, no,

if you'd have kill'd me. Let them that don't believe me, examine the truth of it; may your good angels plague me as I tell ye a lye."

The company were all wondering, when, "Saving what you have said," quoth Trimalchio, "if there be faith in man, my hair stands on end, because I know Niceros is no trifler; he's sure of what he says, and not given to talking: Nay, I'll tell ye as horrible a thing my self; but see there, what's that behind the hangings?"

BOUDA

From Morocco to Angola, the were-hyena is the equivalent of the American and European werewolf. Similar to wolves in that they run in packs, there are many substantial differences besides just how they look.

Hyena packs are always female dominant; the animals evoke a feeling of fear when mentioned but are very undeserving of their monstrous reputation. To say were-hyena in Africa is "Bouda," this name hearkens back to a tribe of people who gained a reputation for being able to shapeshift into a hyena form at will. Unlike their lycan cousins, the ability to make this change is seen as something inherited; there are no curses, or spells, and you cannot be scratched by a shapeshifting hyena to become one. The Bouda's society, much like that of a hyena, is matriarchal and the trait of shapeshifting is passed down from the mother. There are even people who have never heard of the Bouda tribe—merely the word with it's mystical connotations. The Bouda has traveled widely outside of Africa and into the Middle East, Syria, Bulgaria, India, and Turkey.

Common in legends from Morocco to Angola, were-hyenas are surely the African equivalent of the werewolf. Like wolves, hyenas run in packs, and they have been traditionally regarded with great fear, even though the animals themselves are not deserving of their bad reputation. Hyenas do extend further than Africa, and even in Greece, they still carry were-hyena legends.

Hyena as depicted in Aberdeen Bestiary.

HOMBRE LOBO

I will tell you this: If you go to Spain, do not dare utter the word "lobo." There are over seventy other traditional expressions in the language to help avoid saying the word. By saying "lobo" it is believed to summon this horrific entity to you.

Before Spain was conquered by the Romans, the wolf had strong ties to the afterlife as it was common to find them feasting on carcasses of animals and people alike. The Middle Ages were a time of magic and occult powers, and it seemed everybody had these gifts and Hombres Lobo or lobishomes was often a curse the parents unwittingly put upon their children. Such is the case with the story below from the book *Leyendas españolas de todos los tiempos* (*Spanish Legends of All Time*) by José Maria Merino.

> The story goes that a girl from Leon lived with her dad. She loved meat and ate it all of the time. Her lust for this particular food was so bad that one day her father kicked her out of the house and told her to go live with the wolves where she could eat meat all of the time. After her father tossed her out, she could often be seen wandering the Caurel Hills which border El Bierzo. Her dad's comment created a spell which had an immediate effect on her.
>
> That very night, as she was up in the hills, she rolled around on the forest floor and turned into a she-wolf. She traveled across the country, sometimes in the form of a wolf, other times as a woman. Finally, she reached Galicia where she became chieftain of a wolf tribe that caused much damage to the area. When in her wolf form, this tribe decimated the livestock and townsfolk with no concern as to who was harmed. Some believe that when she was in her female form she would build a bon fire to protect the villagers and livestock from her lupine brethren.

One night, the she-wolf went to the miller. She had been there many times before and loved to eat his flour; unlike every other time the miller was actually sleeping at the mill! He was awakened by the sound of a dog pawing at the ground; he looked at the door and saw the paws of a dog trying to get under the door. Knowing that this was no ordinary canine, the miller grabbed his knife and stabbed the animal's paw. There was a terrible howl which turned into a young girl's scream as her wolf hide fell away to reveal her human form.

The miller was astonished by the change and when he began speaking with the girl, she seemed very confused having no idea where she was or what she was doing there. The villagers were enamored by this girl's story and wanted to be able to help her back home. When she did finally return home, she was received very happily by her townsfolk and father.

However, when it was time for harvest and some Galician reapers came by for work, she talked with them and began to remember all of the horrible things she had done as a wolf while she was under her father's spell. She carried this burden with her the rest of her living days.

In Leon and Asturas, people will actually kill the wolves to ward off potential evil caused by the curse of the wolf's gaze, also known as "llobadío." There was such belief among both the Portugese and Spanish countries, that some serial killers native to these areas believed that they, much like the girl in the story, had been cursed by their parents. They actually went on to kill their victims as if they were indeed lobos. However, we will be talking about that later in the book...

IRISH WEREWOLF

Gerald of Wales known by the Latin name Giraldus Cambrensis or the Welsh name Geralt Gymro was an archdeacon of Breacon, and a chronicler. He traveled Wales, and one could say that he was also a dealer in oddities. In his tome the *Topography of Ireland*, he covered everything from a cave that mysteriously filled with wine everyday to a bearded woman. Within that he also notes the experiences of a priest who had a conversation with a he-wolf.

> Around 1173, a priest and his companion were walking from Ulster towards Meath; they made camp, setting up a small fire, when all of a sudden a wolf approached them. The wolf spoke to the two gentlemen saying, "Rest secure, and be not afraid for there is no reason you should fear, where no fear is." The priest and his friend could not believe their ears; the cleric invoked the name of God, calling for protection from the beast and for an understanding of why this animal spoke in human tongue.
>
> The wolf responded to the priest explaining that there were two of them, a man and a woman who came from Ossory and that they'd been cursed by Natalis, the abbot of Ossory, and saint.
>
> The curse ran thusly: Every seven years they were to shed their human form and depart the village of men; if they survived the ordeals, then they were allowed to return to their human form and their community.
>
> But there was a problem. The she-wolf was sick and dying; the he-wolf requested the priest's assistance in giving the she-wolf divine charity by putting upon her the rights of his office. He followed the wolf with more than a tinge of fear; the beast led him to a tree hollow nearby, where the she-wolf lay. A quiet "Thank God" could be heard on a sigh from the female. The priest gave her last communion and upon her supplication, she tried to get the holy man to give her the viaticum (part of the

last rites). He tried to explain how he was not equipped for that ritual. The he wolf who had been trying to give space to his dying friend and the priest came forward at this point. He singled out the small missal-book that the priest held which contained within some consecrated wafers. Then the man-wolf nearly begged the priest to not deny the she-wolf that which Divine Providence had put the priest into her path for. The he-wolf then used one of his large claws to slice the she-wolf's skin from head to belly, folding back the skin, revealing the woman's true form, that of an old woman. Fearful, the priest gave the communion. After it was done, the male wolf refitted the she-wolf's furry layer.

The Werewolf Delusion by Ian Woodard.

Then the he-wolf guided the priest back to his camp staying with him most of the night and acting more human than beast. When morning came, he led the priest to a direct road and thanked him again, promising the priest many great returns when he came out of the Lord's exile. At the end of the conversation, the priest asked about the invaders that had been coming into Ireland and if the wolf felt God would allow them to stay. To this the wolf replied, "For the sins of our nation, and their enormous vices, the anger of the Lord, falling on an evil generation, hath given them into the hands of their enemies. Therefore, as long as this foreign race shall keep the commandments of the Lord, and walk in his ways, it will be secure and invincible; but if, as the downward path of illicit pleasures is easy, and nature is prone to follow vicious examples, this people shall chance, from living among us, to adopt our depraved habits, doubtless they will provoke divine vengeance on themselves also."

Two years later, as Gerald was walking through the same area and was hearing the stories, it happened that a bishop of the area was convening a synod about this particular priest's interactions and how it was to be dealt with. They asked that Gerald come and unfortunately for whatever reason he couldn't make it but send a letter with his suggestion that the priest be seen by the pope bringing letters from those with which he had met.

Gerald goes on into a philosophical questioning as to whether this he-wolf would be considered a brute, as he does think with a man's rational mind. Also, that it was obvious from the tale that yet again, God showed that human nature can be changed to whatever form befits Him.

These negative connotations placed upon the werewolf by Gerald, may just be pieces of political propaganda from a time when Catholics came to bring "order" to a "heathen" land. Before this story, many of the Irish talked of the faoladh of Ossory—they were seen as protective creatures. Although in the old tales it is believed that they could change at will, not that it was a curse and it hearkens back to the shamanic traditions of shapeshifting and astral projection. During the time that a person was a wolf; his or her body would remain at the village as if lifeless. It was said that the body could not be moved because if the wolf could not find its way back to its original incarnation, then it would be stuck in the animal form. They had been known to help lost people find their way, protect children from harm and of course raid cattle, as any good wolf should. However, if he or she was caught or attacked while eating, there would be no attack, rather the wolf form would run away back to its original body.

When the wolf manifestation returned home to its human body the markings of the raid or attack would transfer onto the human's flesh. Blood from livestock, and wounds from a battle never fought while in human form were typical signs that some shapeshifting had occurred.

LOUP GAROU

French for wolf (loup) man (garou), it is also known as Rougarou in Laurentian French communities, this creature is not bound by the phases of the moon but of their own will. The legend says that if someone sheds the blood of the loup garou it will change back into its human form revealing the secret of this beast. The victim, after striking the creature, must serve a term of one hundred and one days as a loup garou; if they tell of their encounter, they will become a loup garou forever. However, if they remain quiet, then after their time, they are able to return back to their families unharmed.

Nowadays though, the loup garou is no longer just contained in France. If you go to heavily French colonized areas in both the United States and Canada, you will find the loup garou legends still thrive.

In Louisiana, the terms Loup Garou and Rougarou are used interchangeably. This wolf is said to prowl the swamps around the New Orleans and Acadian areas. Rougarou, unlike the typical werewolf that we think of, are often seen as having the body of a human, the head of a wolf and claws. Many believe that this legend is much like that of the boogeyman used to keep children and people in line. One of the legends that is often told is that the Rougarou will hunt down misbehaving Catholics during Lent. Here is where the difference lies from the French version. In the original, you hit the loup garou and you change into it; in the Cajun version, if you are struck and blood is drawn, you change.

Whichever is true does not really matter. Either way, you are in trouble if you do and in trouble if you do not.

MUJINA

Much like the kitsune or Tanuki, Mujina (which means badger), it has the ability to take numerous forms. Depending on where you travel, you may find that in one prefect it is called Tanuki; in another it is called Mujina. In parts of the Tochigi Prefecture, the Mujina was used as a term for the raccoon-dog and the badger was Tanuki.

The writer of the following story was an Irishman who in his later years traveled to Japan and fell in love with the country! He penned these stories under the Japanese name Yokumo Koizumi.

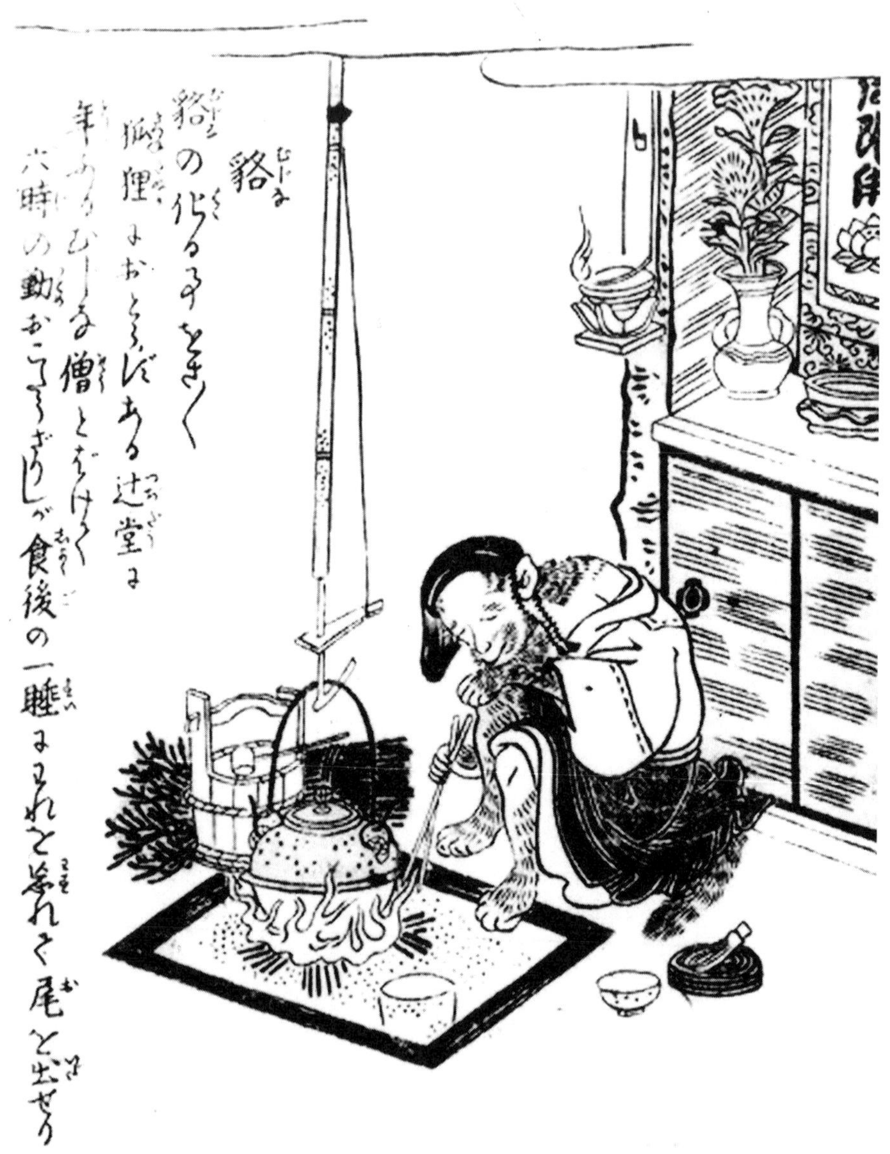

Shapeshifting Mujina from the Konjaku Gazu Zoku Hyakki.

MUJINA

BY LAFCADIO HEARN (KOIZUMI YAKUMO)
FROM KWAIDAN (1904)

On the Akasaka Road, in Tōkyō, there is a slope called Kii-no-kuni-zaka (紀之国坂), which means the Slope of the Province of Kii. I do not know why it is called the Slope of the province of Kii. On one side of this slope you see an ancient moat, deep and very wide, with high green banks rising up to some place of gardens; and on the other side of the road extend the long and lofty walls of an imperial palace. Before the era of street-lamps and jinrikishas (rickshaws), this neighborhood was very lonesome after dark; and belated pedestrians would go miles out of their way rather than mount the Kii-no-kuni-zaka, alone, after sunset.

All because of a Mujina that used to walk there.

Lafacadio Hearn and his wife.

The last man who saw the Mujina was an old merchant of the Kyōbashi Quarter, who died about thirty years ago. This is the story, as he told it:

One night, at a late hour, he was hurrying up the Kii-no-kuni-zaka, when he perceived a woman crouching by the moat, all alone, and weeping bitterly. Fearing that she intended to drown herself, he stopped to offer her any assistance or consolation in his power. She appeared to be a slight and graceful person, handsomely dressed; and her hair was arranged like that of a young girl of good family. "O-jochū," he exclaimed, approaching her, "O-jochū, do not cry like that!... Tell me what the trouble is; and if there be any way to help you, I shall be glad to help you." (He really meant what he said; for he was a very kind man.)

But she continued to weep, hiding her face from him with one of her long sleeves. "O-jochū," he said again, as gently as he could, "please, please listen to me! ... This is no place for a young lady at night! Do not cry, I implore you! Only tell me how I may be of some help to you!"

Slowly she rose up, but turned her back to him, and continued to moan and sob behind her sleeve. He laid his hand lightly upon her shoulder, and pleaded: "O-jochū! O-jochū! O-jochū! Listen to me, just for one little moment! O-jochū! O-jochū!"

Then O-jochū turned round, and dropped her sleeve, and stroked her face with her hand; and the man saw that *she had no eyes or nose or mouth*, and he screamed and ran away.

Up Kii-no-kuni-zaka he ran and ran; and all was black and empty before him. On and on he ran, never daring to look back; and at last he saw a lantern, so far away that it looked like the gleam of a firefly; and he made for it. It proved to be only the lantern of an itinerant soba-seller, who had set down his stand by the road-side; but any light and any human companionship was good after that

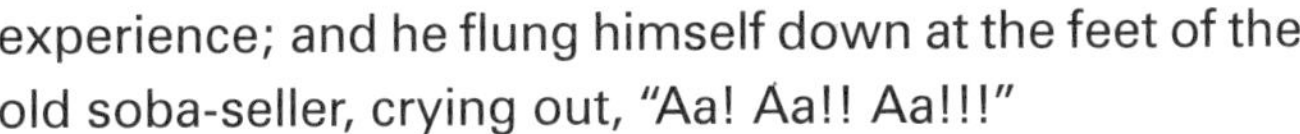

experience; and he flung himself down at the feet of the old soba-seller, crying out, "Aa! Aa!! Aa!!!"

"Kore! Kore!" roughly exclaimed the soba-man. "Here! What is the matter with you? Anybody hurt you?"

"No, nobody hurt me," panted the other, "only... Aa! Aa!"...

"—only scared you?" queried the peddler, unsympathetically. "Robbers?"

"Not robbers, —not robbers," gasped the terrified man... "I saw... I saw a woman—by the moat; —and she showed me... Aa! I cannot tell you what she showed me!"...

"Heh! Was it anything like THIS that she showed you?" cried the soba-man, stroking his own face—, which therewith became like unto an egg...

And, simultaneously, *the light went out*.

O-jochū was a polite term used for addressing a young lady that the speaker does not know.

One of the Mujina's favorite forms is that of a faceless ghost commonly referred to as *noppera-bo.* Most of the stories end with the Mujina wiping its faces off such as the next story. Again these tricksters don't seem to mean any true harm but, unlike the tanuki, they really do like to scare the pants off of ya!

A lazy angler decided that he did not want to have to sit by the river and fish all day, so instead he went to the imperial koi ponds near the Haneiankyo place, which were always well stocked and plentiful. He figured nobody would notice if he got one or two fish from there. His wife upon hearing this warned him not to go forward with his plan, that the pond was considered sacred and located right next to a graveyard! Other anglers reiterate the warning but he is determined.

> So he sat by the pond and while awaiting a nibble on the line he met a beautiful young lady, she too begs him not to fish at the pond. That it is a sacred place and not a place to fish for a day's meal. He ignores her warnings just as he did the other fishermen and his wife. She stands before him and wipes off her face. The man fled the pond and ran back home, where he is confronted by his wife. As she gives him a dressing down for going to the pond and attempting to fish, she too wipes off her face.

So if you go fishing by a sacred koi pond or Kii-no-kuni-zaka and you see a beautiful girl, keep walking. Don't fish and be thankful that you did not upset the mujina.

NAHUAL

This myth is based on the divine celestial calendar of Mesoamerica. Every day has a Nahual connected with it; this is almost like a totem or alter ego for a person and the Nahual helps to direct you in your path. The shapeshifting part comes in later. It is said that a person can "shift" into their Nahual form. These entities will keep guard at night for other Nahual and scare them off. The Nahual of a person is not told to them until they reach an age where the village or culture feels they are responsible enough to handle it. This prevents someone from doing bad deeds and blaming it on the Nahual persona.

In modern Mexico, the spirit of the word has changed to be synonymous with bruja or witch. These women can supposedly shapeshift at night, typically into the forms of a turkey, or an owl. They will then suck the blood of their victims much like a vampire. They are also blamed for spreading disease and stealing property or livestock. Oaxaca, one of the thirty-one states of Mexico, is particularly vulnerable to the witch, Nahual, connection.

Were-jaguars also have connections to the Nahual. The much-revered Aztecs actually had a special force of elite warriors called "Jaguar Warriors" who wore nothing but jaguar skin looking to imbue themselves with the properties of the animal. Shamans would also wear the skins of jaguar as part of their shapeshifting rituals.

In modern times, this myth has been corrupted as people are now seeing were-jaguars along highways similar to the North American tales of vanishing hitchhikers. But along with that, some believe that these shapeshifters are also hired as assassins by the government and cartels.

Q'WAETI "THE TRANSFORMER"

We all know of *Twilight*—love it or hate it. The Quileute Tribe legend Stephanie Meyers touched on is true... Manuel Andrade believes the Quileute have been created by Q'waeti which means *Transformer.* Here is the story as told by a bilingual Quileute named Hallie George and accounted in the book *Quileute Texts*:

> Long ago a man named Q'waeti' traveled across the Olympic Peninsula setting people right and instructing those he met about how to build houses, what would come of the future, and how to model their societies. The animals were not very fond of Q'waeti' and one day the man came upon Beaver, who was sharpening a knife. When Q'waeti' asked Beaver why he was sharpening his knife, Beaver explained that he was going to kill Q'waeti'. The young man grabbed Beaver's knife and stuck it on the animal's tail and deemed that Beaver would always have that knife stuck to its tail. He also commanded that Beaver would live in the water and whenever a human came around, he would *whap* his tail and dive.

Next, he came upon Deer who was sharpening his shell knife and also seemed to have malicious intent regarding Q'waeti'. The hero stuck the shell knife on Deer's ears and told Deer that he would run when frightened, stop, and look back.

Soon after his interaction with Deer, he reached the Q'wayi't'soxk'a River but he didn't find any people. So Q'waeti' spit on his hands and rubbed them together. His dead human skin rubbed off and fell into the water. Where his dead skin fell, people appeared. He told these people that this spot at the river should be their home and their name would be Q'wayi't'sox (Queets).

Q'waeti' then continued on his way until he reached the Hoh people. He saw that these people walked on their hands and carried their nets between their legs. They were called the Upside Down People. They were known as the first people who existed. Q'waeti' went and turned these people right side up and taught them to use their feet to walk and their hands to carry things. He told them to go and fish the smelt at the river, that they would always be plentiful, and since that time, there has always been an abundance of smelt at Hoh.

Q'waeti' continued on until he reached the Quileute lands. There he saw two wolves but no people. Q'waeti' shifted these wolves into humans and instructed these wolf people that each of the members would have only one single wife, but that the chief would be allowed between four and eight. The tribe would be fierce, brave, and strong for they would be descended from wolves.

Q'waeti' continued on, going across the land setting people right, teaching them to hunt, fish, and live a fruitful and productive life. He stopped at the future lands of the Ozette people and there he saw two dogs and changed them into people. Having been dogs, they did not know how to fish, so Q'waeti' taught them to troll for fish on Neah Bay. Since that time, Neah Bay has always been filled with fish.

The Q'waeti' creation mythology is a revered among the Quileute people. Q'waeti' is seen as the guardian of the Quileute people and not one to be taken lightly. It is believed that no wolves will ever be found in the state of Washington because of Q'waeti' and his transformation of

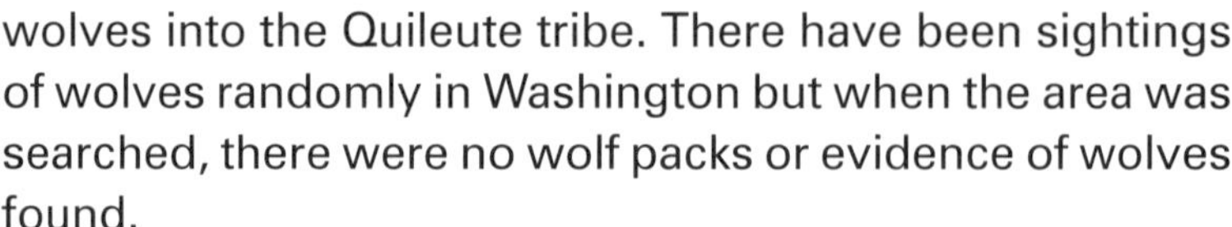

wolves into the Quileute tribe. There have been sightings of wolves randomly in Washington but when the area was searched, there were no wolf packs or evidence of wolves found.

SKINWALKER

Firstly, I want to clear something up: The Skinwalker is not as modern media depicts it. The name within the Navajo tribe is *yee naaldlooshii*, which literally translates to "with it, he walks on four legs" and they are a people who have mastered the art of shapeshifting. These people can shift into any animal they choose—not just the wolf. They can be dangerous, but if you go by the old stories, only to the tribe's enemy, although in the last few hundred years that story has changed.

Throughout history, people have had many encounters with these shapeshifters. Nevertheless, Michael Stuhff, a Las Vegas lawyer, had a very peculiar interaction. While working on a custody case concerning a little boy, things got hairy. One night, the little boy had to spend the night over his father's house; while there the father summoned a medicine man. This person brought with him two wooden dolls; they chanted around the dolls and performed a ritual. When it was done, they buried the two dolls in the cemetery. After the boy came back to his mother's house, he told her what had happened. She had him repeat the story to Michael.

The lawyer then went to a Professor of Navajo culture; he told the professor everything that had happened. The professor informed him that the ritual they performed was to send a skinwalker after him, and the aim was to have both he and the mother end up in the cemetery where the dolls were...dead. The only way to get rid of it was to let it know you knew about it. So Michael went forward and sued both the man and the skinwalker.

The judge presiding over the custody case took this threat very seriously and gave full custody to the mother, forcing the father to pay full child support.

You can tell a real skinwalker by their eyes. They are usually very flat with no real shine to them whatsoever. It is believed that someone who is a skinwalker, when in human form, has a brilliant sheen to their eyes. Also when a skinwalker takes the form of an animal it is usually off just a little bit with its features. Something is always amiss usually within the facial areas.

Robbie Robertson, an indigenous singer, wrote a song entitled "Skinwalker." An short excerpt:

SKINWALKER

A strange encounter to be sure
He was wicked he was pure
Hear him calling, he's calling for you
Come with me into the mystic
Come with me into the night
We can live, live forever
Painted desert, peyote rain
Lord, don't let me go insane.
Skinwalker, skinwalker.

TANUKI

What do Golden Balls, Japan, Super Mario Brothers 3, and teapots have in common? The Tanuki!

Yes, you heard me, the Tanuki are shapeshifting raccoon dogs. As you travel in Japan's Shikiko province you will se an awful lot of statues depicting this big-testicled creature. The entity's large orbs are actually called "Golden Balls" and supposedly bring good fortune in business. This hearkens back to the legends of ancient times where fertility and abundance or prosperity go hand in hand. However, the Tanuki is not as innocent as it looks. It is known for being a mischievous creature. In order to shapeshift it needs a leaf to place upon its head. It can change into people, other animals or inanimate objects. One of the most famous stories called "Bunbuku Chagama" (which translated means "happiness bubbling over like a teapot") is a perfect example of the nature of the Tanuki.

THE ACCOMPLISHED AND LUCKY TEA-KETTLE

A LONG time ago, at a temple called Morinji, in the province of Jôshiu, there was an old tea-kettle. One day, when the priest of the temple was about to hang it over the hearth to boil the water for his tea, to his amazement, the kettle all of a sudden put forth the head and tail of a badger. What a wonderful kettle, to come out all over fur! The priest, thunderstruck, called in the novices of the temple to see the sight; and whilst they were stupidly staring, one suggesting one thing and another, the kettle, jumping up into the air, began flying about the room. More astonished than ever, the priest and his pupils tried to pursue it; but no thief or cat was ever half so sharp as this wonderful badger-kettle. At last, however, they managed to knock it down and secure it; and, holding it in with their united efforts, they forced it into a box, intending to carry it off and throw it away in some distant place, so that they might be no more plagued by the goblin. For this day their troubles were over; but, as luck would have it, the tinker who was in the habit of working for the temple called in, and the priest suddenly bethought him that it was a pity to throw the kettle away for nothing, and that he might as well get a trifle for it, no matter how small. So he brought out the kettle, which had resumed its former shape and had got rid of its head and tail, and showed it to the tinker.

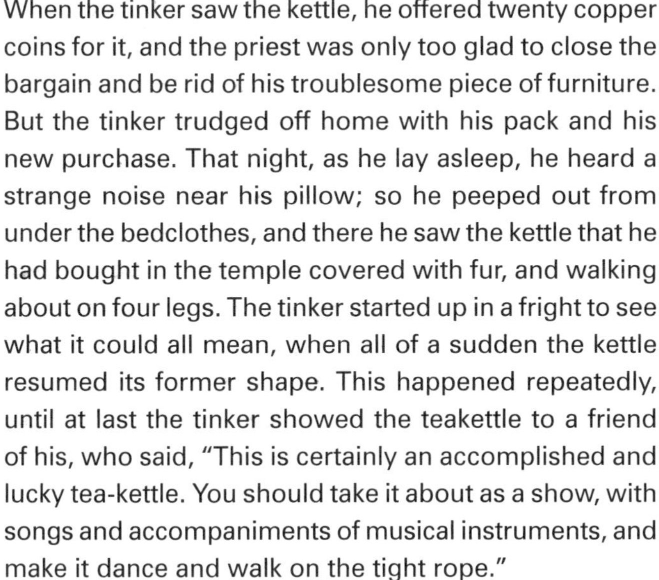

> When the tinker saw the kettle, he offered twenty copper coins for it, and the priest was only too glad to close the bargain and be rid of his troublesome piece of furniture. But the tinker trudged off home with his pack and his new purchase. That night, as he lay asleep, he heard a strange noise near his pillow; so he peeped out from under the bedclothes, and there he saw the kettle that he had bought in the temple covered with fur, and walking about on four legs. The tinker started up in a fright to see what it could all mean, when all of a sudden the kettle resumed its former shape. This happened repeatedly, until at last the tinker showed the teakettle to a friend of his, who said, "This is certainly an accomplished and lucky tea-kettle. You should take it about as a show, with songs and accompaniments of musical instruments, and make it dance and walk on the tight rope."
>
> The tinker, thinking this good advice, made arrangements with a showman, and set up an exhibition. The noise of the kettle's performances soon spread abroad, until even the princes of the land sent to order the tinker to come to them; and he grew rich beyond all his expectations. Even the princesses, too, and the great ladies of the court, took great delight in the dancing kettle, so that no sooner had it shown its tricks in one place than it was time for them to keep some other engagement. At last the tinker grew so rich that he took the kettle back to the temple, where it was laid up as a precious treasure, and worshipped as a saint.

The Morinji Temple in Tatebayashi in the Gunma Prefecture is about an hour and a half plane ride from Asakusa and approximately sixty-two miles from Tokyo. This is the place where the story took place; if you go to the temple, you will see about twenty-five or thirty of these raccoon-dog sculptures lining the way. Morinji

Temple prides themselves in the story and take great care of the Takuni, but the tale does not end there. The Takuni's testicles are so famous that even children sing about them!

Tan Tan Tanuki no kintama wa,
Kaze mo nai no ni,
Bura bura

The Tan- Tan- Tanuki's testicles are,
Despite there being no wind blowing,
Swaying, swaying, swaying.

Even the video games have incorporated takuni into their plot lines. In Super Mario Brothers 3, Mario is able to gather falling leaves, and when he does, he magically gains the "Takooni" suit which allows him to fly! Thank goodness, the inventors decided not to follow the legendary form of the takuni to the letter!

There are some takuni stories, which look to vilify this trickster, one of which is the story of Kachi-Kachi Yama retold as Kachi-Kachi Mountain in the *Japanese Fairy-Tale Series* (Vol. 1 Issue 5).

KACHI-KACHI MOUNTAIN

Once upon a time there was an old farmer who cultivated a field in the mountains. One day his old wife came and brought him his dinner, but a badger stole and ate it. This made the old man angry and at last, he took the badger alive, carried it home with him, and hung it to a rafter by the feet. Then he said to his wife "Let us have this badger for soup. Have it well cooked and wait till I come back." Then he went again to the field. His wife was

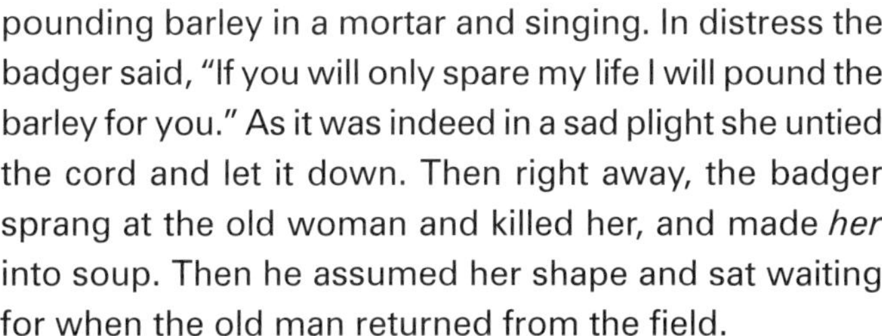

pounding barley in a mortar and singing. In distress the badger said, "If you will only spare my life I will pound the barley for you." As it was indeed in a sad plight she untied the cord and let it down. Then right away, the badger sprang at the old woman and killed her, and made *her* into soup. Then he assumed her shape and sat waiting for when the old man returned from the field.

When he was about to partake of the soup, the badger assumed his original form, and cried out, "You wife-eating old man you! Did not you see the bones under the floor?" Laughing derisively, it escaped out of doors and disappeared. The old man threw down his chopsticks and cried long and bitterly. Now in the same mountain there lived an old rabbit. Hearing the voice of the old man crying, he came and tried to comfort him, and said he would himself avenge the death of the old woman,

"First," he said, "parch me some beans." And the old man parched them. The rabbit put the parched beans in a pouch and said, "Now to the mountain again;" and away he went. The badger was attracted by the smell, and came out and said; "Give me about a handful of those beans. This was what the rabbit was expecting. So he said, "I will if you will carry a bundle of dry-grass for me over to yon mountain."

"I will do as you say without fail," replied the badger, "Only first give me the beans."

He begged importunately, but the rabbit said, "Yes, after you have carried the load of dry-grass."

He then put on his back a great pile of dried-grass and sent the badger on before, while he took out his flint and struck out a spark, and set the bundle on fire. The badger alarmed at the noise asked, "What is that?" The rabbit replied; "that is Kachi-Kachi mountain." Soon the fire began to kindle and spread in the dried-grass.

> The badger hearing this again asked, "What is that?" The rabbit replied, "That is Bo-Bo mountain." By this time, the fire had spread to the badger's back and burnt it badly. Crying out in pain, he rolled over, shook off his load, and ran away out of sight. The rabbit next mixed some sauce and red pepper and made a sticking plaster, put on a hat and set out to sell it as a cure for blisters and burns. The badger was then lying helpless with his back all ray and sore. That must be good medicine, he thought, when he heard of it. So he got some applied to his back. But there is not language to tell how he smarted when the red-pepper sticking plaster was applied to his sore skin. He just rolled over and over and howled long and bitterly. Now after about twenty days the badger's sore was healed.
>
> The rabbit was then making a boat and the badger seeing it asked, "What are you going to do with this boat?" The rabbit replied, "I intend to catch fish." Thus deceiving. The badger felt envious, but was dull in that kind of work.
>
> "I will make a boat of clay," he said. So having made a clay boat he rowed out to sea along with the rabbit. Then the badger's boat began to sink, and when it was sinking, the rabbit brandished aloft his oar and struck the badger dead, thus avenging the old man's wife.

This is one, if not the only truly negative, story of the tanuki that I have been able to find. It was during the Kamakura and Muromachi eras that these sinister stories about these amazing creatures began to circulate. Tanuki is prized and featured not just in woodcuts, art, and storytelling but also in the kitchen in the form of Tanuki-jiru or Tanuki Soup.

TANUKI-JIRU OR TANUKI SOUP

HERE IS WHAT YOU NEED:

1/2 pound of tanuki (or pork/rabbit substitute)
1 parsnip, peeled
4 inches of daikon (Japanese radish)
6 shiitake mushrooms, whole
1 package of firm tofu
4 cups of dashi stock
1/4 cup of barley miso
2-3 green onions
1 1/2 tbsp. sesame oil

Cut your tanuki into small pieces and brown it in the sesame oil, over a medium flame. The best thing to use is a wok.

Brown the tanuki, but not all the way through. Remember this is a soup, so it will continue to cook in the stock and helps to keep the meat tender. Deglaze it with 1 cup of dashi stock.

In an earthenware pot with a lid, add the meat and juice. Add an additional cup of the dashi stock, the parsnip, daikon, mushrooms and tofu. Cover the pot with the lid and simmer for 15-30 minutes or until the daikon is transparent.

In a separate bowl, add miso and the last two cups of dashi; keep mixing till it gets smooth, then add them to the simmering pot, keep it cooking for another 5-8 minutes.

Slice the green onions into little circles and add them to the pot for a dash of extra flavor and nice presentation. Serve.

Overall the tanuki are usually somewhat gullible and absent-minded creatures. To recognize the tanuki (aside from the large testicles), there are some other telltale signs that what you are seeing is a tanuki. They have very big eyes, always wear a bamboo hat and carry a sake bottle. Their tails are very big and they carry a promissory note. They also have a very large belly and always wear a smile. These distinguishing characteristics are hallmarks for the tanuki. If you come across one in your travels, please let me know.

WENDIGO

Stories and descriptions of the Wendigo vary from tribe to tribe as does the spelling of this beast (some spell it *windigo* or *weendigo* among other versions). Rugaru is also mentioned by the Native American tribes which lay on the Canadian border. Some believe that these are two names for the same being, however author Peter Mathiessen disagrees. He says that they are two completely separate legends and that the Ojibwe may have picked it up from French traders. It seems that the natives actually revere the Rugaru and it bears more of a resemblance to Sasquatch as they are seen as being in tune with Mother Earth and nature. Whereas with the Wendigo are hungry for human meat and blood. Everything within the indigenous communities is passed on through oral traditions, so overtime stories blend and change. However, there is one thing that has always been consistent, in order for one to become a wendigo, you must first become a cannibal. There was one other way and that was to become possessed by the spirit of a wendigo, usually happening during a dream state.

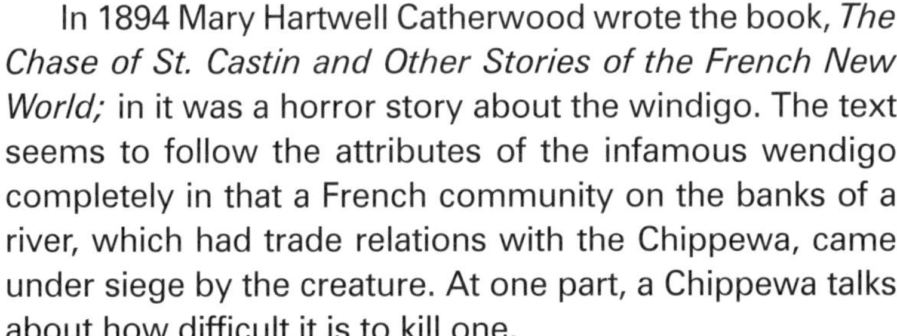

In 1894 Mary Hartwell Catherwood wrote the book, *The Chase of St. Castin and Other Stories of the French New World;* in it was a horror story about the windigo. The text seems to follow the attributes of the infamous wendigo completely in that a French community on the banks of a river, which had trade relations with the Chippewa, came under siege by the creature. At one part, a Chippewa talks about how difficult it is to kill one.

> " He will not want to go to the lodges anymore after dark."
>
> The widow remarked, noting Michel's fat legs and arms, "Windigo like to eat him."
>
> "I would kill a windigo," declared Michel, in full revolt.
>
> "Not so easy to kill a windigo. Bad spirits help windigos. If man kill windigo and not tear him to pieces, he come to life again."
>
> Archange herself shuddered at such a tenacious creature. She was less superstitious than the Chippewa woman, but the Northwest had its human terrors as dark as the shadow of witchcraft.
>
> Though a Chippewa was bound to dip his hand in the war kettle and taste the flesh of enemies after victory, there was nothing he considered more horrible than a confirmed cannibal. He believed that a person who had eaten human flesh to satisfy hunger was never afterwards contented with any other kind, and, being deranged and possessed by the spirit of a beast, he had to be killed for the safety of the community. The cannibal usually became what he was by stress of starvation: in the winter when hunting failed and he was far from help, or on a journey when provisions gave out, and his only choice was to eat a companion or die. But this did not excuse him. As soon as he was detected, the name of "windigo" was given him, and if he did not betake himself again to solitude he was shot or knocked on the head at the first convenient opportunity. Archange remembered one such wretched

creature who had haunted the settlement awhile, and then disappeared. His canoe was known, and when it hovered even distantly on the river, every child ran to its mother.

Later they have an encounter with the wendigo and give account of a disturbing appearance. They use plenty of descriptive words and if you have any imagination, it will be easily pictured.

"There was no one. Michel is here." Archange snatched the curtain aside, and leaned out to see the orphan sprawled on a bearskin in front of the collapsing logs. He had pushed the sashes inward from the gallery and hoisted himself over the high sill after the bed drapery was closed for the night, for the window yet stood open.

Madame Cadotte sheltered the candle she carried, but the wind blew it out. There was a rich glow from the fireplace upon Michel's stuffed legs and arms, his cheeks, and the full parted lips through which his breath audibly flowed. The other end of the room, lacking the candle, was in shadow.

The thump of the Indian drum could still be heard, and distinctly and more distinctly, as if they were approaching the house, the rapids.

Both women heard more. They had not noticed any voice at the window when they were speaking themselves, but some offensive thing scented the wind, and they heard, hoarsely spoken in Chippewa from the gallery,

"How fat he is!"

Archange, with a gasp, threw herself upon her mother-in-law for safety, and Madame Cadotte put both arms and the smoking candle around her. A feeble yet dexterous scramble on the sill resulted in something dropping into the room. It moved toward the hearth glow, a gaunt vertebrate body scarcely expanded by ribs, but covered by a red blanket and a head with deathlike

> features overhung by strips of hair. This vision of famine leaned forward and indented Michel with one finger, croaking again,
>
> "How fat he is!"
>
> The boy roused himself, and, for one instant stupid and apologetic, was going to sit up and whine. He saw what bent over him, and, bristling with unimaginable revolutions of arms and legs, he yelled a yell which seemed to sweep the thing back through the window.

In the end the Chippewa started to hunt the wendigo because Archange and the rest of the community thought it ate her husband. This proved to be untrue, as he had decided to take a canoe and be on his own for bit (bad timing on his part). They ended up finding the wendigo and followed her across the river, where they finally captured her. They killed her and buried her right on the spot.

WERE-RAT

Part of the reason I am including the were-rat is that I think it does not get enough press. It is one of those curious little-looked-at cryptids. Nevertheless with such things as were-bears, werewolves, were-cats, and more, who is going to pay attention to the mere were-rat.

According to myths, oftentimes, these were witches who kept rats as familiars and would change into the rat form at will. There are not many legends of the were-rat although Brad Steiger did cover some sightings in Oregon, mostly reported by children. There is said to be a large community of were-rats in Pennsylvania. Dungeons and Dragons as well as other fantasy board and video games have made a name for the were-rat as an evil nasty creature that likes to bite flesh. Although from what I have come to understand, they are strictly vegetarian, unless there is dead meat nearby...Then they might nibble...just a little bit. Were-rats do possess the ability to control the other rats around them, to lead them, and instruct them. So if you see a mob of rats coming your way led by a really big one...running would not be a bad idea.

WERE-VAMPIRE

Nowadays we are used to seeing vampires and werewolves as archenemies but in old Slavic cultures these two creatures were commonly mixed together. In Slavic culture varkolak (meaning wolf's fur), some of the legends say that the wolf being is actually a ghost or a vampire. But most agree that it is truly what the name indicates, a werewolf. Much like Fenrir from the Norse legends, this werewolf can swallow the Sun in its powerful jaws, however in some cultures they are believed to come from the corpses of babies.

FOLKLORE AND FURRY TAILS

Stories, both oral and written make up much of our superstitions and mythology. I love reading the old tales about werewolves and shapeshifters—not all of them being bad or horrible by any means.

WERE-BRIDES AND FAMILY TAILS

There are many myths recounting animal brides. But this one is one of my favorites, hearkening from Croatia, it was written about in 1889 by A.H. Wraitslaw in the book *Sixty Folk-Tales from Exclusively Slavonic Sources.*

THE SHE-WOLF - CROATIA

There was an enchanted mill, so that no one could stay there, because a she-wolf always haunted it. A soldier went once into the mill to sleep. He made a fire in the parlor, went up into the garret above, bored a hole with an auger in the floor, and peeped down into the parlor.

A she-wolf came in and looked about the mill to see whether she could find anything to eat. She found nothing, and then went to the fire, and said, "Skin down! Skin down! Skin down!" She raised herself upon her hind-legs, and her skin fell down. She took the skin, and hung it on a peg, and out of the wolf came a damsel. The damsel went to the fire, and fell asleep there.

German Werewolf
woodcut, 1722

German woodcut of a werewolf transforming 1722.

He came down from the garret, took the skin, nailed it fast to the mill-wheel, then came into the mill, shouted over to her, and said, "Good morning, damsel! How do you do?"

She began to scream, "Skin on me! Skin on me! Skin on me!" But the skin could not come down, for it was fast nailed.

The pair married and had two children.

As soon as the elder son got to know that his mother was a wolf, he said to her, "Mamma! Mamma! I have heard that you are a wolf."

His mother replied, "What nonsense are you talking! How can you say that I am a wolf?"

The father of the two children went one day into the field to plow, and his son said, "Papa, let me, too, go with you."

His father said, "Come."

When they had come to the field, the son asked his father, "Papa, is it true that our mother is a wolf?"

The father said, "It is."

The son inquired, "And where is her skin?"

His father said, "There it is, on the mill-wheel."

No sooner had the son got home, than he said at once to his mother, "Mamma! Mamma! You are a wolf! I know where your skin is."

His mother asked him, "Where is my skin?"

He said, "There, on the mill-wheel."

His mother said to him, "Thank you, sonny, for rescuing me." Then she went away, and was never heard of more.

THE WEREWOLF'S DAUGHTER - SLOVAKIA

This tale flew through Slovakia and right into Sabine-Baring-Gould's book *The Book of Werewolves: Being an Account of a Terrible Superstition* back in 1865.

There was once a father, who had nine daughters, and they were all marriageable, but the youngest was the most beautiful.

The father was a werewolf. One day it came into his head, "What is the good of having to support so many girls?" So he was determined to put them all out of the way.

He went accordingly into the forest to hew wood, and he ordered his daughters to let one of them bring him his dinner. It was the eldest who brought it.

"Why, how come you so early with the food?" asked the woodcutter.

"Truly, father, I wished to strengthen you, lest you should fall upon us, if famished!"

"A good lass! Sit down whilst I eat."

He ate, and whilst he ate he thought of a scheme. He rose and said, "My girl, come, and I will show you a pit I have been digging."

"And what is the pit for?"

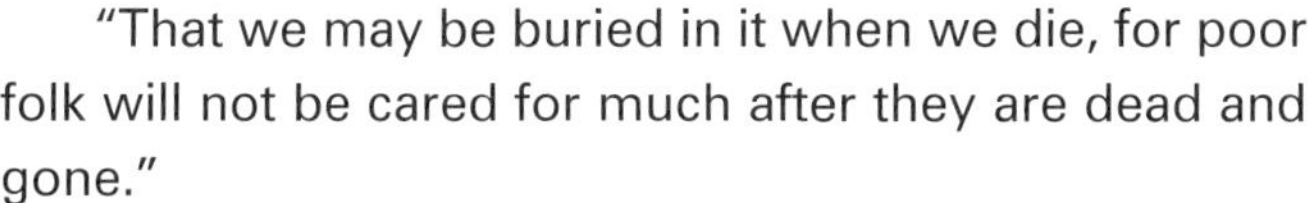

"That we may be buried in it when we die, for poor folk will not be cared for much after they are dead and gone."

Therefore, the girl went with him to the side of the deep pit.

"Now hear," said the werewolf. "You must die and be cast in there."

She begged for her life, but all in vain. So he laid hold of her and cast her into the grave. Then he took a great stone and flung it in upon her and crushed her head, so the poor thing breathed out her soul. When the werewolf had done this he went back to his work, and as dusk came on, the second daughter arrived, bringing him food. He told her of the pit, and brought her to it, and cast her in, and killed her as the first. And so he dealt with all his girls, up to the last.

The youngest knew well that her father was a werewolf, and she was grieved that her sisters did not return. She thought, "Now where can they be? Has my father kept them for companionship, or to help him in his work?"

So she made the food which she was to take him, and crept cautiously through the wood. When she came near the place where her father worked, she heard his strokes felling timber, and smelt smoke. She saw presently a large fire and two human heads roasting at it. Turning from the fire, she went in the direction of the ax strokes and found her father.

"See," said she. "Father, I have brought you food."

"That is a good lass," said he. "Now stack the wood for me whilst I eat."

"But where are my sisters?" she asked.

"Down in yon valley drawing wood," he replied. "Follow me, and I will bring you to them."

They came to the pit. Then he told her that he had dug it for a grave. "Now," said he, "you must die, and be cast into the pit with your sisters."

"Turn aside, father," she asked, "whilst I strip off my clothes, and then slay me if you will."

He turned aside as she requested, and then—tchich! She gave him a push, and he tumbled headlong into the hole he had dug for her. She fled for her life, for the werewolf was not injured, and he soon would scramble out of the pit.

Now she hears his howls resounding through the gloomy alleys of the forest, and swift as the wind she runs. She hears the tramp of his approaching feet, and the snuffle of his breath. Then she casts behind her handkerchief. The werewolf seizes this with teeth and nails, and rends it until it is reduced to tiny ribands. In another moment, he is again in pursuit foaming at the mouth, and howling dismally, whilst his red eyes gleam like burning coals. As he gains on her, she casts behind her gown, and bids him tear that. He seizes the gown and rives it to shreds, then again he pursues. This time she casts behind her, her apron, next her petticoat, then her shift, and at last runs much in the condition in which she was born. Again, the werewolf approaches. She bounds out of the forest into a hay field and hides herself in the smallest heap of hay. Her father enters the field, runs howling about it in search of her, cannot find her, and begins to upset the different haycocks, all the while growling and gnashing his gleaming white fangs in his rage at her having escaped him. The foam flakes drop at every step from his mouth, and his skin is reeking with sweat. Before he has reached the smallest bundle of hay, his strength leaves him. He feels exhaustion begin to creep over him, and he retires to the forest.

The king goes out hunting every day. One of his dogs carries food to the hay field, which has most unaccountably been neglected by the haymakers for three days. The king, following the dog, discovers the fair damsel, not exactly "in the straw," but up to her neck in hay. She is carried, hay and all, to the palace, where she becomes his wife, making only one stipulation before becoming his bride, and that is, that no beggar shall be permitted to enter the palace.

After some years, a beggar does get in, the beggar being, of course, none other than her werewolf father. He steals upstairs, enters the nursery, cuts the throats of the two children borne by the queen to her lord, and lays the knife under her pillow.

In the morning, the king, supposing his wife to be the murderess, drives her from home, with the dead princes hung about her neck. A hermit comes to the rescue, and restores the babies to life. The king finds out his mistake, is reunited to the lady out of the hay, and the werewolf is cast off a high cliff into the sea, and that is the end of him.

The king, the queen, and the princes live happily, and may be living yet, for no notice of their death has appeared in the newspaper.

THE WOMAN WHO BECAME A HORSE – OKANĀ'QĒN TRIBE

Native Americans are one of those cultures who have some of the best myths going, the Okanā'qēn tribe located along the Canadian border and into British Columbia had this wonderful story about a woman who turned into a horse. Unlike most were-beast stories once the transformation happens it is permanent, but is still a good show of therianthropy.

A chief had many horses, and among them a stallion which his wife often rode. The woman and stallion became enamored of each other and cohabited. The woman grew careless of her household duties and always wanted to look after the horses.

When the people moved camp, and the horses were brought in, it was noticed that the stallion made right for the woman and sniffed about her as stallions do with mares. After this, she was watched.

When her husband learned the truth, he shot the stallion. The woman cried and would not go to bed.

At daybreak she was gone, no one knew where. About a year after this it was discovered that she had gone off with some wild horses. One day when the people were traveling over a large open place they saw a band of horses, and the woman among them. She had partly changed into a horse. Her pubic hair had grown so long that it resembled a tail. She also had much hair on her body, and the hair of her head had grown to resemble a horse's mane. Her arms and legs had also changed considerably; but her face was still human, and bore some resemblance to her original self.

The chief sent some young men to chase her. All the wild horses ran away, but she could not run so fast as they, and was run down and lassoed. She was brought into her husband's lodge; and the people watched her for some time, trying to tame her, but she continued to act and whinny like a horse. At last they let her free. The following year they saw her again. She had become almost entirely horse, and had a colt by her side. She had many children afterwards.

THE MAN WHO MARRIED A BEAR – NEZ PERCÉ

Some animals in Native American lore have supernatural abilities besides just the shapeshifting. In this particular story (a love story), you will find that our were-bear can tell the future.

A man named Five-Times-Surrounded-in-War (Pákatamápaütx) lived with his father at Asotin, and in the spring of the year the youth would go away from home and lose himself till fall. He would tell no one where he had been. Now, he really was accustomed to going up the Little Salmon (Hune'he) branch of the Grande Ronde River to fish for salmon. It was the second year that he went there that this thing happened.

A bear girl lived just below the forks of Asotin Creek, and from that place she used to go over onto the Little Salmon, where Five-Times-Surrounded-in-War had a camp made of boughs. One day, after fishing, he was lying in his camp not quite asleep. He heard the noise of someone walking in the woods. He heard the noise of walking go all around the camp. The grizzly-bear girl was afraid to go near the man, and soon she went away and left him. Next morning he tried to track her; and while he could see the tracks in the grass, he could not tell what it was that made them.

Next day the youth hunted deer in order to have dried meat for the winter; and that evening the grizzly-bear girl, dressed up as a human being, came into his camp. Five-Times-Surrounded-in-War had just finished his supper when he heard the footfalls, and, looking out into the forest, he saw a fine girl come into the open. He wondered if this person was what he had heard the night before.

He asked the girl to tell him what she wanted, and she came and sat down beside him. The youth was bashful and could not talk to her, although she was a pretty girl. Then he said, "Where are you camping?" And she told him that three days before she had come from the forks of Asotin Creek.

"I came to see you, and to find out whether or not you would marry me."

Now, Five-Times-Surrounded-in-War did not know of anyone who lived above the mouth of Asotin Creek, and for that reason he told the girl he would take home his meat and salmon and return in ten days. So the girl went back to the forks of Asotin Creek, and the youth to the mouth of the stream with his meat. Then they returned and met; and the youth fell deeply in love with the girl, and married her.

So they lived in his camp until she said to him, "Now we will go to my home."

And when they arrived, he saw that she had a fine supply of winter food —dried salmon, dried meat, camas, *kaus*, *sanitx*, serviceberries, and huckleberries. However, what most surprised him was that they went into a hole in the ground, because then he knew she must be a bear.

It grew late in the fall, and they had to stay in the cave, for the girl could not go out. In the dead of winter, they were still in the cave when the snow began to settle and harden. One night, near midnight, when both were asleep in their beds, the grizzly-bear girl dreamed, and roared out in her sleep.

She told her husband to build a fire and make a light. Then the grizzly-bear girl sang a song, and blood came running from her mouth. She said, "This blood you see coming from my mouth is not my blood. It is the blood of men. Down at the mouth of Asotin Creek the hunters are making ready for a bear hunt. They have observed this cave, and five hunters are coming here to see if a bear is in it." The grizzly-bear girl in her sleep knew that the hunters were making ready.

Next morning the five hunters went up to that place, and that same morning the grizzly-bear girl donned a different dress from what she usually wore, a dress that was painted red. She told her husband, "Soon after the sun leaves the earth, these hunters will be here, and then I will do my killing."

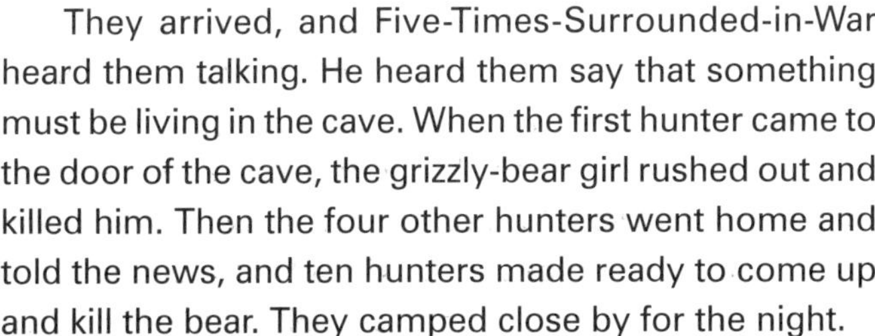

They arrived, and Five-Times-Surrounded-in-War heard them talking. He heard them say that something must be living in the cave. When the first hunter came to the door of the cave, the grizzly-bear girl rushed out and killed him. Then the four other hunters went home and told the news, and ten hunters made ready to come up and kill the bear. They camped close by for the night.

About midnight the grizzly-bear girl had another dream. She sang a song, and told her husband, "I will leave you as soon as the sun is up. This blood you see coming out of my mouth is my own blood. The hunters are close by, and will soon be here."

Soon the youth could hear the hunters talking. Then they took a pole and hung an empty garment near the mouth of the cave, and the bear rushed out at this decoy. When she turned to go back, they fired, and killed her.

The youth in the cave heard the hunters say, "Watch out! There must be another one in the cave."

So he decided he would go out; and when he came into the light, the hunters recognized him. He went home with them and told the story.

This was the year before the French trappers came, and Five-Times-Surrounded-in-War went away with them. In a year, he returned, and after that he disappeared.

WEREWOLF WAR STORIES

WEREWOLF OF BETTEMBOURG

This German tale carries all the components of a really good horror story. It's short but well worth the read.

A long time ago, an old and crippled soldier came from the direction of Luxembourg City. He lay down to rest at a cross standing on a hill just outside the town of Bettembourg.

Suddenly he jumped to his feet, started swearing to God and Hell, and completely destroyed the representation of our Lord's crucifixion.

From that day, a big wolf started haunting the grounds around the old church of Bettembourg, killing all that would come in his way. No bullet and no spear could do him any harm, until a wise monk told the people of Bettembourg to make a bullet of silver into which to carve the names of Jesus, Maria, and Joseph.

The hunters then set out to track the beast and eventually shot it. When they arrived at the place it had disappeared, and the body they found, was that of the old soldier, who turned out to be a former Bettembourgian.

On this hill, a small cross still stands, and sometimes at night, howling wolves can still be heard near it.

THE BATTLE OF HAFSFJORD

The Norse really loved their stories of battle and none were better nor more dangerous than the berserker (ber meaning "bear" and serkr "coat" or berr "skin" serkr "shirt") and the *ulfheðinn (wolf coats).*

They would go to battle wearing nothing but the skins of either the bear or the wolf believing that they carried with them the properties of the animal, becoming the animal. They were driven into a frenzy and could withstand pain to the umpteenth degree, including swallowing hot coals. It is also believed that the berserker could dull a blade by looking at it, and that their coats deflected any edged weapon, and that iron never harmed them. Here is an account of a battle in which the berserkers and ulfheðinn fought as edited and translated by N. Kershaw for Cambridge University Press in 1922.

Oscar Montelius, Om lifvet i sverige under hednatiden (Stockholm 1905) s.8. Translated: About Life in Sweden During Pagan Times.

Hearken how the king of noble lineage fought yonder in Hafsfjord against Kjotvi the wealthy. A fleet came from the east, with gaping figure-heads and carved beaks—impelled by desire for battle. They were laden with warriors and white shields, with spears from the West and swords from France. The berserks were howling, the "wolf-coats" were yelling, and swords were clashing: Their warfare was in full swing. They made trial of the resolute monarch of the men of the east, who dwells at Utsteinn.

He pointed them the road to flight. The king brought out his ocean steeds when he had a prospect of battle. There was a clashing of shields ere Haklangr fell. Then the thick-necked chief showed no inclination to maintain his land against the Shock-head. He used the island as a shield. Those who were wounded thrust themselves under the benches, arching their backs and pushing their heads down into the keel. The prudent warriors took care to cover their backs with glittering shields—the shingles of Othin's hall—as they were pelted with stones. Their prows were in headlong flight towards the east, and homewards from HafsQord they fled by way of JaSarr, with their minds set on the meadcups.

WITCHES AND SHAPESHIFTING

Witches' most common form was that of a cat, surprised? Not really. Cats have had long associations with witches as familiars. However, with most of these folktales, it ends with the hero harming the animal that sneaks into their house or room and then waking up the next morning or that evening and seeing the mark of the witch.

THE TWO CAT WITCHES - WALES

In old days, it was believed that the seventh son, in a family of sons, was a conjurer by nature. That is, he could work wonders like the fairies and excel the doctors in curing diseases.

If he were the seventh son of a seventh son, he was himself a wonder of wonders. The story ran that he could even cure the "shingles," which is a very troublesome disease. It is called also by a Latin name, which means a snake, because, as it gets worse, it coils itself around the body.

Now the eagle can attack the serpent, conquer, and kill this poisonous creature. To secure such power, Hugh, the conjurer, ate the flesh of eagles. When he wished to cure the serpent disease, he uttered words in the form of a charm, which acted as a talisman and cure.

After wetting the red rash, which had broken out over the sick person's body, he muttered,

"He-eagle, she-eagle, I send you over nine seas, and over nine mountains, and over nine acres of moor and fen, where no dog shall bark, no cow low, and no eagle shall higher rise."

After that, the patient was sure that he felt better.

There was always great rivalry between these conjurers and those who made money from the pilgrims at holy wells and visitors to the relic shrines, but this fellow, named Hugh, and the monks, kept on mutually good terms. They often ate dinner together, for Hugh was a great traveler over the whole country and always had news to tell to the holy brothers who lived in cells.

One night, as he was eating supper at an inn, four men came in and sat down at the table with him. By his magical power, Hugh knew that they were robbers and meant to kill him that night, in order to get his money.

So, to divert their attention, Hugh made something like a horn to grow up out of the table, and then laid a spell on the robbers, so that they were kept gazing at the curious thing all night long, while he went to bed and slept soundly.

When he rose in the morning, he paid his bill and went away, while the robbers were still gazing at the horn. Only when the officers arrived to take them to prison did they come to themselves.

Now at Bettws-y-Coed—that pretty place which has a name that sounds so funny to some of us and suggests a girl named Betty the Co-ed at college—there was a hotel, named the "Inn of Three Kegs." The shop sign hung out in front. It was a bunch of grapes gilded and set below three small barrels.

This inn was kept by two respectable ladies, who were sisters.

Yet in that very hotel, several travelers, while they were asleep, had been robbed of their money. They could not blame anyone nor tell how the mischief was done. With the key in the keyhole, they had kept their doors locked during the night. They were sure that no one had entered the room. There were no signs of men's boots, or of anyone's footsteps in the garden, while nothing was visible on the lock or door, to show that either had been tampered with. Everything was in order as when they went to bed.

Some people doubted their stories, but when they applied to Hugh the conjurer, he believed them and volunteered to solve the mystery. His motto was "Go anywhere and everywhere, but catch the thief."

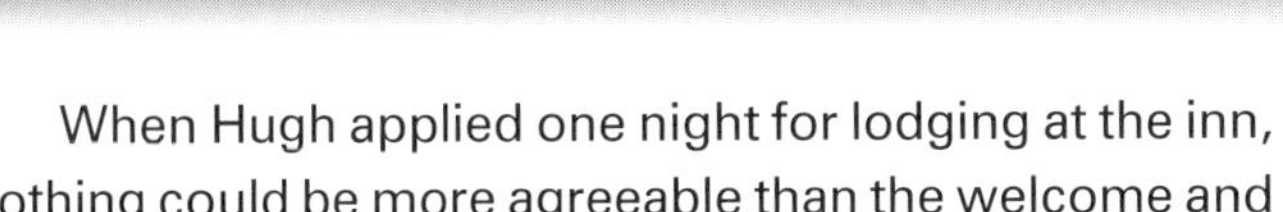

When Hugh applied one night for lodging at the inn, nothing could be more agreeable than the welcome and fine manners of his two hostesses.

At suppertime, and during the evening, they all chatted together merrily. Hugh, who was never at a loss for news or stories, told about the various kinds of people and the many countries he had visited, in imagination, just as if he had seen them all, though he had never set foot outside of Wales.

When he was ready to go to bed, he said to the ladies, "It is my custom to keep a light burning in my room, all night, but I will not ask for candles, for I have enough to last me until sunrise." So saying, he bade them good night.

Entering his room and locking the door, he undressed, but laid his clothes near at hand. He drew his trusty sword out of its sheath and laid it upon the bed beside him, where he could quickly grasp it. Then he pretended to be asleep and even snored.

It was not long before, peeping between his eyelids, only half closed; he saw two cats come stealthily down the chimney.

When in the room, the animals frisked about, and then gamboled and romped in the liveliest way. Then they chased each other around the bed, as if they were trying to find out whether Hugh was asleep.

Meanwhile, the supposed sleeper kept perfectly motionless. Soon the two cats came over to his clothes and one of them put her paw into the pocket that contained his purse.

At this, with one sweep of his sword, Hugh struck at the cat's paw. The beast howled frightfully, and both animals ran for the chimney and disappeared. After that, everything was quiet until breakfast time.

At the table, only one of the sisters was present. Hugh politely inquired after the other one. He was told that she was not well, for which Hugh said he was very sorry.

After the meal, Hugh declared he must say good-bye to both the sisters, whose company he had so enjoyed the night before. In spite of the other lady's many excuses, he was admitted to the sick lady's room.

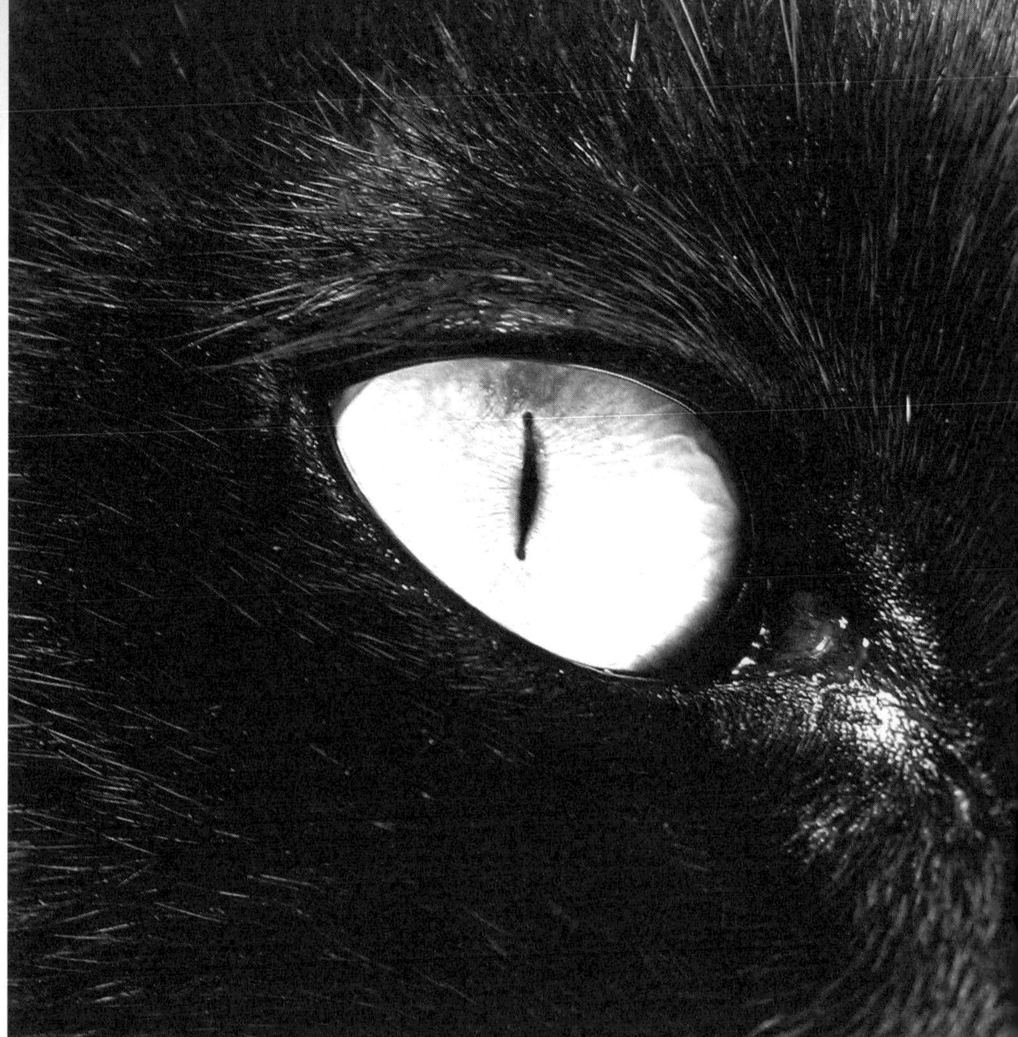

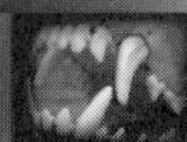

After polite greetings and mutual compliments, Hugh offered his hand to say "good-by." The sick lady smiled at once and put out her hand, but it was her left one.

"Oh, no," said Hugh, with a laugh. "I never in all my life have taken anyone's left hand, and, beautiful as yours is, I won't break my habit by beginning now and here."

Reluctantly, and as if in pain, the sick woman put out her hand. It was bandaged.

The mystery was now cleared up. The two sisters were cats. By the help of bad fairies, they had changed their forms and were the real robbers.

Hugh seized the hand of the other sister and made a little cut in it, from which a few drops of blood flowed, but the spell was over.

"Henceforth," said Hugh, "you are both harmless, and I trust you will both be honest women."

And they were. From that day, they were like other women, and kept one of the best of those inns—clean, tidy, comfortable, and at modest prices—for which Wales is, or was, noted.

Neither as cats with paws, nor landladies, with soaring bills, did they ever rob travelers again.

A WITCH IS RECOGNIZED – GERMANY

Whenever a certain peasant brewed beer, someone drank it all up during the night. He finally decided to stay up and keep watch throughout the night.

He did this, and as he was standing by his vat, a large number of cats approached him. He called out to them:

Here kitty,
Here cat,
Come and warm yourselves!

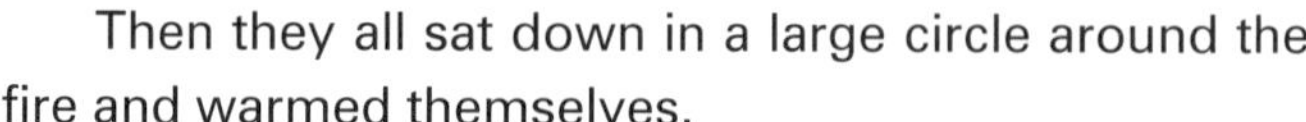

Then they all sat down in a large circle around the fire and warmed themselves.

After they had sat there for a little while, he asked them if the water was hot.

"It is almost boiling!" they answered, and as soon as they said this, he took the ladle and sprinkled the whole lot of them, whereupon they all disappeared in an instant.

The next day his wife had a badly burned face, so he knew who had been drinking up his beer.

A WITCH AS WEREWOLF – GERMANY

Once a witch was crossing a field in the form of a werewolf in order to bewitch a farmer's cows. Her husband came upon her, and when he saw the wolf, he was afraid that it might be his wife, so he called out, "Marie, Marie, what are you doing here?"

This frightened the woman, who turned herself back into her human form. But even as the man approached her, long red hair was still hanging from her neck and breast, and her eyes were still glowing like wolf's eyes.

HERODOTUS AND THE LAND OF THE SHAPESHIFTERS

A fifth-century Greek historian, Herodotus, was allowed much adventuring and wandering during his day. He is often looked at as the "Father of History" in the western world, the title first being given to him by Cicero. However, unlike many historians, he did like to add a little flourish to his stories, and since writing them, some of the tales have proven to be just that. Herodotus maintained throughout

the writing that he was just jotting down information that he had overheard or that had been told to him. It would seem that Herodotus gathered much in the way of negative attention for his supposed accurate histories. In epigraph in Thuria, one of three places where Herodotus is believed to be buried, it reads:

Herodotus the son of Lyxes here
Lies; in Ionic history without peer;
A Dorian born, who fled from Slander's brand
And made in Thuria his new native land

In his tome, *The History of Herodotus,* he speaks of a people with a very intriguing ability. Read the excerpt below:

> The Neurian customs are like the Scythian. One generation before the attack of Darius they were driven from their land by a huge multitude of serpents which invaded them. Of these some were produced in their own country, while others, and those by far the greater number, came in from the deserts on the north. Suffering grievously beneath this scourge, they quitted their homes, and took refuge with the Budini. It seems that these people are conjurers: for both the Scythians and the Greeks who dwell in Scythia say that every Neurian once a year becomes a wolf for a few days, at the end of which time he is restored to his proper shape. Not that I believe this, but they constantly affirm it to be true, and are even ready to back their assertion with an oath.

Of course he gives no credence whatsoever to the idea of a people who change into wolves annually. However, this could be a reference to shamanic practices which at times incorporate the act of shapeshifting.

WEREWOLVES IN MODERN MEDIA

In earlier days, our folklore was brought to us through the grapevine, word of mouth, or the reading of a book. I remember when I sat down with Laurie Cabot (founder of the Cabot tradition based out of Salem, Massachusetts) for my book *Witches and Witchcraft in the 21st Century*; she expressed to me the importance of maintaining the oral tradition. Every time I would ask her a question, she would answer it with a story; it was one of my favorite interviews. In today's modern society, with televisions, movies, audio books, Internet, the Ipad, and smart phones, our world keeps getting smaller, and information spreads more rapidly than ever before. This also means the way our folklore spreads is much different than *back in the day*. Today our modern tales are told to most of us through the television, movies, audio books and web pages we read.

However, I have, and always will, love a good ghoulish campfire story. To illustrate this point, I recruited my friend, Don Smith, Jr., a comic book writer, to discuss the evolution of the werewolf mythos in the graphic novel industry. We will also explore the werewolf icon through television and movies!

WEREWOLVES IN COMIC BOOKS

BY DON E. SMITH JR.

"Werewolf!"
"Werewolf?"
"There."
"What?"
"There, wolf. There, castle."
"Why are you talking that way?"
"I thought you wanted to."
"No, I don't want to."
"Suit yourself. I'm easy."

Young Frankenstein (1974)
~An exchange between characters:
Inga, Dr. Frederick Frankenstein, and Igor

HOWL!

In his 1865 work, *The Book of Were-Wolves*, writer Sabine Baring-Gould said that lycanthropy was the "change of man or woman into the form of a wolf, either through magical means, so as to enable him or her to gratify the taste for human flesh, or through judgment of the gods in punishment for some great offence."

Illustration by Sandra Lanz
Courtesy of Saint James Comics Ex Occultus

In the world of comic books, the werewolf is right at home. Just the very nature of a "change of man or woman" into something bestial and primitive is right out of the Incredible Hulk. The man/beast combination was popularized with a certain Dark Knight detective seeking to avenge the death of his mother and father by a petty criminal. Using Baring-Gould's definition with gods and magic, heck, even the "gratify the taste for human flesh," these are elements that fit into a good old-fashioned comic book.

The first "real" comic book appeared in 1929 which was a reprint of newspaper comic strips put in a tabloid-sized format. But it was not popularized until 1938 when Superman leapt over "a tall building in a single bound" in *Action Comics* #1. Since then, comic books have been called an art form as unique as jazz or the Western. With the amount of horror anthologies in the 1950s, like *Tales from the Crypt* or *Vault of Terror*, stories of werewolves (more or less the same style of monster as Lon Chaney Jr.'s *The Wolf Man*) would appear in single issue adventures. However, that was almost not to be thanks to an overreaching psychiatrist named Frederic Wertham with his 1954 book *Seduction of the Innocent*. He blamed many of the ills that young boys faced on comic books. *Seduction* criticized super heroes like Batman and Robin, Superman, and Wonder Woman for their actions depicting situations as metaphors for deviant behavior. However, much of his criticism was aimed at EC Comics, published by Bill Gaines (who went on to publish *Mad* Magazine) with titles like *Tales from the Crypt*, *The Haunt of Fear* and *The Vault of Horror*. Considering these were anthology series, each of them had a handful of werewolf stories.

However, to prevent the United States government from dictating the content of comic books, the industry adopted the Comics Code Authority, which offered a list

of guidelines as to *what* and *whatnot* could be printed in a comic book. According to the preamble of the code:

> The comic-book medium, having come of age on the American cultural scene, must measure up to its responsibilities and constantly improving techniques and higher standards go hand in hand with these responsibilities [and] to make a positive contribution to contemporary life, the industry must seek new areas for developing sound, wholesome entertainment. The people responsible for writing, drawing, printing, publishing, and selling comic books have done a commendable job in the past, and have been striving toward this goal.

One of the edicts adopted was, "Scenes dealing with, or instruments associated with walking dead, torture, vampires and vampirism, ghouls, cannibalism, and werewolfism are prohibited" putting the silver bullet through the heart of the werewolf in comic books. However, when the code was updated in 1971, the ghoulish spirits and monsters of the night were allowed to return to the pages of comic books—specifically, Marvel Comics (the same people who gave us Iron Man, Spider-Man, and Captain America) introduced Jack Russell as the *Werewolf By Night*. The *Werewolf by Night* featured Russell, a man who discovered his family's curse, or as it said at the beginning of every issue, "The tag's Russell, with a Jack in front of it. The kind of name that fits a normal 19-year-old dude living out in L.A.—not the kind of name you'd expect to find slapped on a guy who sprouted fangs, pore-to-pore fur, and a wolfish howl every time the moon ballooned full." Most of the series was Russell seeking a cure for his sister who was about to turn 18 years old. In his series, he met Marvel Comics stalwarts Iron Man, Frankenstein's monster, Brother Voodoo, and the

Moon Knight. Russell first appeared in *Marvel Spotlight #2* and was created by Gerry Conway and Mike Ploog. But it was a bit of a challenge because, in comic books, vampires have had a longer life than werewolves.

"I heard someone say vampire myth is based on seduction, whereas the werewolf myth is based on rape," said comic book writer Gerry Conway. He said much of the reason werewolves were relegated to a "comic book limbo" was because of the Comics Code Authority. "In 1971, as the Comics Code Authority changed the rules about what could and could not be done in a story, Marvel decided to do a line of comics featuring monsters," said Conway. He added, "Up until then, Marvel would use giant or Japanese-style monsters, but with the Comics Code restrictions lifted we were able to focus on creatures like Dracula, Frankenstein's monster and the wolf-man." He explained that Marvel Comics' editor at the time, Roy Thomas, contributed much to the origin of the *Werewolf By Night*, along with his wife at the time, Jean Thomas. When asked if it was on purpose the protagonist was named Jack Russell, as in the dog breed, Conway laughed. "I don't think it was intentional, but I can see how that can be inferred," said Conway Regarding Russell's appearance, which was similar to the Lon Chaney style of werewolf, Conway said the visual look of the character was the responsibility of the artist. "The artistic choice and design fell to Mike Ploog," said Conway.

Ploog had drawn for other Marvel titles like Man-Thing, Ghost Rider, and The Monster of Frankenstein. Conway said he was happy to work with Ploog on the comic. "Werewolves had a very limited history in comic books," said Conway. "There were so many different versions of the vampire story in film and literature, but there really had been only one important version of the werewolf and that was the Larry Talbot character from *The Wolf Man*

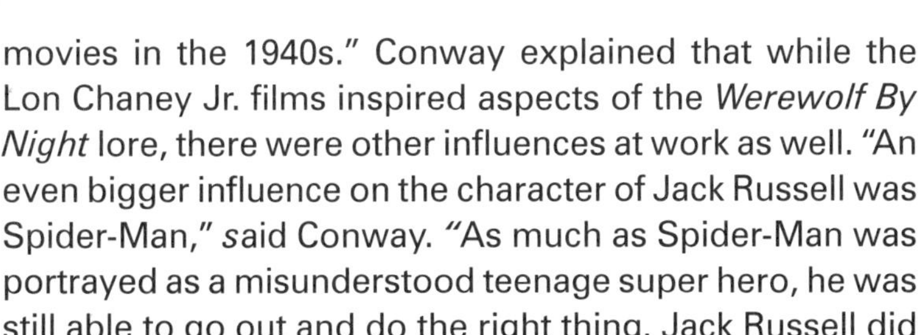

movies in the 1940s." Conway explained that while the Lon Chaney Jr. films inspired aspects of the *Werewolf By Night* lore, there were other influences at work as well. "An even bigger influence on the character of Jack Russell was Spider-Man," said Conway. "As much as Spider-Man was portrayed as a misunderstood teenage super hero, he was still able to go out and do the right thing. Jack Russell did not have that luxury, because essentially he'd turn into a mindless monster that could harm another person."

When asked why the werewolf legend has endured for as long as it has, Conway explained that it's just good old-fashioned story telling. "I think it really boils down to story," said Conway. "Does it have a good hook? Is it iconic? Is there an emotional element readers can relate to?" He explained that while the werewolf movie, *The Howling*, had "uneven special effects," it still told a good werewolf story. "The story was told in an amusing way," he said. "But on a personal, character level, it portrayed the pain experienced by the innocent victim of the werewolf curse, and as a viewer, you can feel that."

But ultimately, Conway praised the screenwriter of the 1941 movie *The Wolf Man* for his work. "Werewolves were difficult to translate to the printed page before screenwriter Curt Siodmak," he said. "When it comes to the modern image of the werewolf as a tortured soul, we have him to thank." Add to the fun of Marvel Comics, Marvel has a mythology plotted out for their characters that is as in depth as anything found in the Bible. For example, this is taken from the Marvel Universe's entry on the "werewolf" as it appears within the Marvel Universe:

> The story of werewolves begins with the ancient Wolf God/Demon, believed to be one of the Elderspawn, the children of the Elder Gods. Millions, possibly billions, of years ago, the Wolf Demon spawned a race of Wolf-

> Men who warred against other Elderspawn such as the Bird-Women, Harpies, Bat-Men, Flying Fiends, Demons, Goblins, Serpent Men (spawn of the Elder God Set), and Spider-Men (spawn of Omm). Some of these races enslaved the developing humans, but by 20,000 B.C., most of the Elderspawn had been slaughtered or driven into seclusion, briefly rising to challenge societies such as Valusia and Atlantis. The Wolf-Men could assume human form, and humans scratched or bitten by them became Wolf-Men in turn. They could survive most injuries, but were vulnerable to silver and fire. Many Wolf-Men died in the Great Cataclysm of 18,000 B.C., and their ultimate fate is unknown.

In DC Comics, werewolves have appeared in issues of *Sandman*, and werewolves were the stars of the title *High Moon* which were displayed at Zuda Comics (a subset of DC Comics). According to the plot summary:

> Former Pinkerton detective Matthew Macgregor investigates a slew of strange happenings in the town of Blest, Texas, a town parched by drought, stricken with famine and haunted by werewolves. As Macgregor attempts to unravel the secrets of Blest, he struggles to contain the secret of his own supernatural past...a struggle that will continue to haunt him across the plains of the American West.

Also in DC's title *Fables*, the Big Bad Wolf steps out of a fairy tale land and is a detective called Bigby Wolf and he solves crimes from fairy tale-themed villains. In 2008, Image Comics introduced *The Astounding Wolf-Man* by Robert Kirkman, with art by Jason Howard. According to their first issue, Gary Hampton was camping when he was attacked by a strange beast. He wakes up in the hospital a month after. When the full moon hits, he turns into a werewolf similar in style to the types of werewolves seen in the *Underworld* movies, but white. He is able to

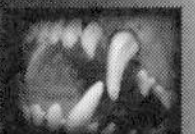

channel his "animal tendencies" into a more super hero style form. Moonstone Comics released two titles *Werewolf the Apocalypse* and *Werewolves: The Call of the Wild*. According to Moonstone's site, *The Call of the Wild* features a tale of revenge as it says, "If you're going to kill a man, you best make sure his brother won't come looking for him. Especially if that man's brother is a werewolf."

Werewolves have appeared in other comic books like *Hellboy* and *Judge Dredd,* of course in recent years, lyncanthropic man-beasts are the subject of independent comic book creators. The independent company Saint James Press introduced werewolves in the first issue of their comic *Ex Occultus*. *Ex Occultus* is a "globetrotting, serialized epic combining elements of Indiana Jones, H. P. Lovecraft, and *The X-Files* as it follows the exploits of adventurer and fortune-hunter Francis Wakefield, the gruff and grizzled Englishman with a tortuous past, and his protégé, a young man only known as Hollander, as they journey through the arcane in search of treasures and fortune, righting wrongs as they go."

Illustration by Sandra Lanz. *Courtesy of Saint James Comics.*

"There are so many fantastic creatures and myths from all over the world, but from the very beginning I knew I wanted to do a more classic monster tale, something fairly familiar. I mean, we were basically creating this brand new series and asking people to join us, so it made sense to use something people would have some knowledge of," said series writer Robert James Russell. "At the same time, though, I wanted to do something wholly original, and when I got the idea of using Celtic mythology to tell a werewolf story, something that, to my knowledge, hadn't been done before, I couldn't resist." He added, "Personally, I love the whole 'tortured soul' element of werewolves—that oftentimes, these people are a slave to this metamorphosis, not actively embracing the dark side like vampires and ghouls and whatnot. Even in our story, our wolves are bad, sure, but they have motivations for their actions, making them more sympathetic as they search for redemption, a way to break their curse. You don't get that with a lot of vampire stories – once they're turned, there's not much they can do about it. Here, we have the wolves trying to actively change who they are and I think it makes them a bit more relatable to the reader (even though they're the bad guys)."

The first issue, entitled *The Badge of Langavat,* chose to focus away from gypsies, but a Celtic route.

"The Celtic route happened more by chance more than anything. After I decided I wanted to do a story featuring werewolves, I came across a little known Scottish myth claiming that at one time wolfmen lived near Loch Langavat in the Outer Hebrides of Scotland," said Russell. "It went on to say that, even though now extinct, if their graves were ever disturbed, their spirits would be released. I did quite a bit more digging and couldn't find much more information than this, but the idea of having Celtic werewolves seemed like such an original prospect, and it painted this fantastic

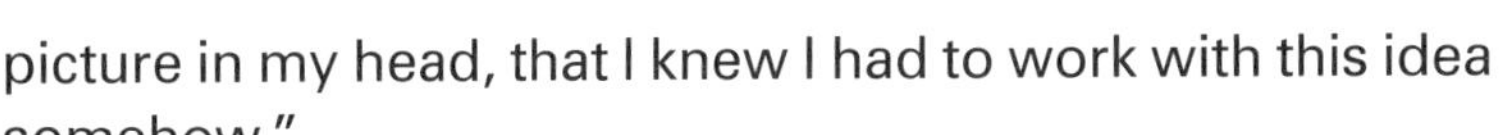

picture in my head, that I knew I had to work with this idea somehow."

Russell further explained, "Celtic mythology is very rich, so I took the little information I had about these werewolves and crafted it into a larger, more elaborate myth involving a once-prominent family who slighted a powerful Druid who eventually cursed them into becoming these werewolves. Again, I think the whole idea of using Celtic mythology was just too good to pass up, and gave me the chance to be a bit over the top and still be grounded in believable histories." Russell said the style of werewolf used was dictated by the story. "The idea of using Celtic mythology was just too good to pass up. It's so rich and distinct, the first thing that popped into my head was: 'They have to be wearing kilts or sashes or something.' And we did just that. For this specific story, the idea is that these werewolves are terrorizing local villages, trying to find children to sacrifice to Celtic gods in order to regain their human forms, and it made more sense for them to be a blend of wolf and human, like they're trying to hold on to their previous lives any way they can—walking on two legs, still wearing clothes, living in the ruins of their once-grand estate," said Russell.

Russell reasoned why he thought werewolves were popular today. "I think there's a human element to werewolves you don't get with other mythological creatures—I mean, they are, in fact, humans who go through a metamorphosis to become wolves (unlike vampires who are just vampires and no longer humans)." He further added, "I think it's fascinating, though, the way werewolves are presented in popular culture. The past few years have given us the *Twilight, Underworld, True Blood, Harry Potter, and the Prisoner of Azkaban*—not to mention, various comics and novels. It's no shock that people like to be scared, and beyond this human element that I personally think makes werewolves more appealing, they're just scary as hell. They represent this carnal version of man acting on instinct to kill and eat, and, depending on your source material, wake up the next day and don't remember anything. They are a slave to their actions and I think that resonates deep with audiences."

Russell said fans can expect to see more werewolf stories. "I also think there are more original stories to tell with werewolves. You can go the whole tortured soul route featuring an innocent person who has no control over his/her actions (i.e., *An American Werewolf in London),* or you can go the 'bad guys who embrace their wolf side' (i.e., the *Underworld* films). It just seems like there are more options for original storytelling with werewolves than with other creatures, and I think that attracts creators, artists, and eventually audiences."

In 2009, comic book creator Rob Brown published his comic *Bane of the Werewolf* through Silver Phoenix Entertainment. With just over 2,000 copies sold, Brown was surprised when the independent comic "took home the Screamie" at the 2009 Horror Comic Awards for Best Artist and Best Inker. Readers became aware that Brown knew his way around the famed were-beast. "I think werewolves have gotten away from their [cinematic] roots," said Rob Brown in a telephone interview. "It seems now werewolves have become something similar to the wolves you see in the *Underworld* movies." Brown said that his comic was a chance to "re-establish the werewolf back into its classic gypsy-type roots. I wanted *Bane of the Werewolf* to have the feel of the old Hammer movies, Bela Lugosi films, the Universal Horror monsters, and through it instill a visual modern twist," he said. In issue one of *Bane*, according to the Silver Phoenix website, "A gypsy vagabond, Eliphas Moreau, rediscovers his past and learns the dark secret his gypsy guardian has been trying to keep from him – a curse that has caught up with him and now must be released

for the sake of all. The werewolf Eliphas confronts the hunchback Olund in a monster-clash that must be seen to be believed."

"Being a werewolf is being cursed," he said. "A lot of people have forgotten that."

When asked why he went the direction of the lyncathrope, he explained that in recent years, other horror icons have been overdone (case in point, the vampire). "Frankly, the zombies have been, pardon the pun, done to death," he said. "I do have vampires and the Frankenstein monster appearing in the five issue series, but it is told from the point of view of the werewolf." The werewolf that Eliphas becomes is similar to what Oliver Reed portrayed in the 1961 Hammer film *The Curse of the Werewolf.* "I'm a big classic horror fan, and *The Curse of the Werewolf* is one of my favorite movies," said Brown. "I wanted the werewolf Eliphas to reflect that type of character." Considering he discussed the *Underworld* movies and discussed his style of werewolf, Brown was asked when the "dog man" style of werewolves appeared.

Bane the Werewolf by Rob Brown. *Courtesy of Rob Brown.*

"Don't hold me to this, but I believe it was artist Frank Franzetta who began to popularize that style of werewolf. The image that comes to mind is the cover for Creepy #4," said Brown. "But I prefer the more human featured style of werewolf because it allows the reader to put himself into the position of the monster." Brown also speculated on why the werewolf remains such an icon. "We make choices every day as to whether we will do something good or something bad," said Brown. "I think the werewolf represents that dark side of the human condition and every so often it is fun just to let it out and play."

Yet Bluewater Comics did a twist on the werewolf in comic book form with *The Puppy Sister*. *The Puppy Sister* was a 1995 novel written by S.E. Hinton, of *The Outsiders* fame and, according to Hinton's website:

> Aleasha the puppy loves her new family. Mom and Dad Davidson smell friendly, and they laugh a lot. And though Nick would have preferred a sister to an unruly pup, he can usually be coaxed to play...Still, Aleasha wants to play human games with Nick and to eat at the table with the family. Worse, she doesn't even look like her family, and Miss Kitty tells her that she'll never become a person. But Aleasha won't give up without trying. She has a most amazing plan.

Darren Davis, the publisher of Bluewater met with Hinton, and had the book adapted into a graphic novel, by me. "S.E. Hinton, was and still is, one of the most popular and best known writers of young adult fiction and now she comes to graphic novels in this touching family story," said Davis. "I think *The Puppy Sister* can be considering a 'reverse werewolf story' and told with the same sense of fun that Michael J. Fox had when he portrayed his teenage werewolf in *Teen Wolf*," said Davis.

Davis added that re-imagining werewolf stories is like "re-telling the old Greek myths. "We re-tell those Greek myths but with comic books," said Davis. He explained that

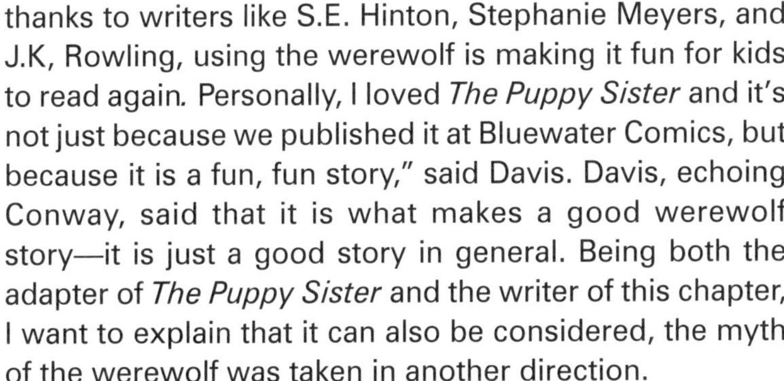

thanks to writers like S.E. Hinton, Stephanie Meyers, and J.K, Rowling, using the werewolf is making it fun for kids to read again. Personally, I loved *The Puppy Sister* and it's not just because we published it at Bluewater Comics, but because it is a fun, fun story," said Davis. Davis, echoing Conway, said that it is what makes a good werewolf story—it is just a good story in general. Being both the adapter of *The Puppy Sister* and the writer of this chapter, I want to explain that it can also be considered, the myth of the werewolf was taken in another direction.

"*The Puppy Sister* is a story told by Aleasha, an Australian Shepherd, who loves her brother Nick, her mom and dad so much that she turns into a human being," I said in an interview with the Jazma Online comic book news site. Whereas the other fantastic stories of people being cursed to turn into a beast, Aleasha's story is, as I explained, "the miracle of love. If you love someone so deeply, or love anything that deeply, you can do the impossible, such as change species....Aleasha had so much love for her brother Nick and parents, she wanted to be more in their lives than just the dog who chases, fetches, and sleeps in the laundry room."

However, like in the movies, werewolves will always have a home in comic books.

DON'S ACKNOWLEDGMENTS

For this chapter, I could not have written it without the help of some amazing people.

First, thank you to Katie Boyd for allowing me this chance. *Second*, thank you to the great Gerry Conway for his time. *Third*, thank you to Rob Brown for his time and providing art for this section. Please visit his site at www.Baneofthewerewolf.com and check out his amazing comic book.

Fourthly, thanks to the Robert James Russell and Jesse Young for their patience and playing phone tag with me. Also thank you to them for providing the art drawn by the amazing Sandra Lanz. Please visit their site at www.whoissaintjames.com and see what the future of comic books looks like.

Fifth, I want to thank Darren Davis, the publisher of Bluewater Comics for his time. In addition, by default, thank you, Ms. Hinton, for both the chance to adapt your amazing story. Credit for the art goes to the amazing Ramon Salas and amazing Mike Miller.

TELEVISION AND MOVIES

"People want to know why I do this, why I write such gross stuff. I like to tell them that I have the heart of a small boy—and I keep it in a jar on my desk."

~Stephen King

During the year 1913, a silent movie (all of eighteen minutes in length) came out called *The Werewolves*, based on the story written by Henry Beaugrand in 1898. Unfortunately, no remaining copy of the original movie exists due to a fire at the Universal Studios in 1924. What a shame, because seeing the difference on how werewolf movies have progressed since the 1900s, would have been neat. Over time, hundreds of so-called werewolf movies have been made, but again I will mention one of my favorites called *Silver Bullet (1985)* which was based on the novel called *Cycle of the Werewolf* written by Stephen King. It had that strange humor yet thrill mixed into the movie, just a fun movie all around in my opinion and stuck to that simple myth that werewolves can die from a silver bullet. Nevertheless, here is a full listing of movies ranging from the first werewolf movie all the way up into the year 2011. (I really did not realize there were so many movies, that had been made on the subject.)

1. *The Werewolf* (1913)
2. *Le Loup-Garou* (1923)
3. *Wolf Blood* (1925)
4. *Le Loup Garou aka Werewolf* (1932)
5. *Werewolf of London* (1935)
6. *The Wolf Man* (1941)
7. *The Mad Monster* (1942)
8. *The Undying Monster* (1942)
9. *Le Loup des Malveneur* (1943)
10. *Frankenstein Meets the Wolf Man* (1943)
11. *Cry of the Werewolf* (1944)
12. *The Return of the Vampire* (1944)
13. *House of Frankenstein* (1944)
14. *House of Dracula* (1945)
15. *She-Wolf of London* (1946)
16. *Abbott and Costello Meet Frankenstein* (1948)
17. *The Werewolf* (1956)
18. *El Castillo de los Monstruos* (1957)
19. *I Was a Teenage Werewolf* (1957)
20. *How to Make a Monster* (1958)
21. *La Casa del Terror* (1959)
22. *The Curse of the Werewolf* (1961)
23. *Lycanthropus* (1962)
24. *Face of the Screaming Werewolf* (1964)
25. *La Loba* (1964)
26. *Dr. Terror's House of Horrors* (1965)
27. *Mad Monster Party* (1967)
28. *Return from the Past* (1967)
29. *La Marca del Hombre Lobo* (1967)
30. *Las Noches del Hombre Lobo* (1968)
31. *Blood of Dracula's Castle* (1969)
32. *Nympho Werewolf* (1970)
33. *Los Monstruos del Terror* (1970)
34. *Werewolves on Wheels* (1971)
35. *Homem Lobo* (1971)
36. *La Noche de Walpurgis* (1971)
37. *La Furia del Hombre Lobo* (1972)
38. *Dr. Jekyll y el Hombre Lobo* (1972)
39. *El Retorno de Walpurgis* (1973)
40. *The Werewolf of Washington* (1973)
41. *The Boy Who Cried Werewolf* (1973)
42. *The Beast Must Die* (1974)

43.	*La Maldicion de la Bestia*	(1975)
44.	*La Bête*	(1975)
45.	*Legend of the Werewolf*	(1975)
46.	*The Werewolf of Woodstock*	(1975)
47.	*La Lupa Mannara*	(1976)
48.	*Wolfman*	(1979)
49.	*El Retorno del Hombre Lobo*	(1980)
50.	*Full Moon High*	(1981)
51.	*The Howling*	(1981)
52.	*An American Werewolf in London*	(1981)
53.	*Wolfen*	(1981)
54.	*La Bestia y la Espada Magica*	(1983)
55.	*Monster Dog*	(1984)
56.	*The Company of Wolves*	(1984)
57.	Howling II: Stirba – Werewolf Bitch	(1985)
58.	*Silver Bullet*	(1985)
59.	*Ladyhawke*	(1985)
60.	*Teen Wolf*	(1985)
61.	*Transylvania 6-5000*	(1985)
62.	*Howling III: The Marsupials*	(1987)
63.	*Teen Wolf Too*	(1987)
64.	*The Monster Squad*	(1987)
65.	*Howling IV: The Original Nightmare*	(1988)
66.	*Curse of the Queerwolf*	(1988)
67.	*My Mom's A Werewolf*	(1989)
68.	*Howling V: The Rebirth*	(1989)
69.	*Howling VI: The Freaks*	(1991)
70.	*Wolfman – A Cinematic Scrapbook*	(1991)
71.	*Mad at the Moon*	(1992)
72.	*Full Eclipse*	(1993)
73.	*Wolf*	(1994)
74.	*Conrad Brooks vs. the Werewolf*	(1994)
75.	*Howling: New Moon Rising*	(1995)
76.	Project: Metalbeast	(1995)
77.	*Shriek of the Lycanthrope*	(1995)
78.	*Licántropo*	(1996)
79.	*Bad Moon*	(1996)
80.	*Werewolf*	(1996)
81.	*Wilderness*	(1996)
82.	*An American Werewolf in Paris*	(1997)

83.	*Tale of The Urban Werewolf*	(1997)
84.	*The Werewolf Reborn!*	(1998)
85.	*Lycanthrophobia*	(1998)
86.	*The Wolves of Kromer*	(1998)
87.	*Lycanthrope*	(1999)
88.	*Eyes of the Werewolf*	(1999)
89.	*Alvin and the Chipmunks Meet the Wolfman*	(2000)
90.	*Ginger Snaps*	(2000)
91.	*Dog Soldiers*	(2002)
92.	*Wolves of Wall Street*	(2002)
93.	*Big Fish*	(2003)
94.	*Underworld*	(2003)
95.	*Tomb of the Werewolf*	(2003)
96.	*Ginger Snaps 2: Unleashed*	(2004)
97.	*Harry Potter and the Prisoner of Azkaban*	(2004)
98.	*Van Helsing*	(2004)
99.	Cursed	(2005)
100.	*The Beast of Bray Road*	(2005)
101.	*The Werewolf Cult Chronicles: Vietnam 1969*	(2005)
102.	*Wallace and Gromit and The Curse of The Were-Rabbit*	(2005)
103.	*Wild Country*	(2005)
104.	*The Brothers Grimm*	(2005)
105.	*Ginger Snaps Back*	(2005)
106.	*Underworld: Evolution*	(2006)
107.	*Big Bad Wolf*	(2006)
108.	*The Feeding*	(2006)
109.	*Bloodz vs Wolvez*	(2006)
110.	*Lycanthropy*	(2006)
111.	*Werewolf in a Women's Prison*	(2006)
112.	*Blood and Chocolate*	(2007)
113.	*The Lycanthrope*	(2007)
114.	*Skinwalkers*	(2007)
115.	*The Devil's Hound*	(2007)
116.	*Benighted*	(2008)
117.	*Freeborn*	(2008)
118.	*In the Blood*	(2008)
119.	Never Cry Werewolf	(2008)
120.	*Twilight*	(2008)
121.	*Underworld: Rise of the Lycans*	(2009)
122.	*War Wolves*	(2009)

123.	*Full Moon Fever*	(2009)
124.	*New Moon*	(2009)
125.	*Hotel Transylvania*	(2009)
126.	*Human*	(2010)
127.	*The Wolfman*	(2010)
128.	*Eclipse*	(2010)
129.	*An American Werewolf in Paris*	(2011)
130.	*Attack of The Lycan*	(2011)
131.	*Red Riding Hood*	(2011)

Even in the world of television, the werewolf in worming it's way into the plot lines of major cable shows, and even inspiring new ones! The popular television show, *Tru Blood* (2008 when show first aired) season three introduces the audience to a new character which is a werewolf. And *The Gates* (2010 first air date) also has the mix of vampires, demons, and werewolves. Today, avid fans of television and the paranormal have accepted these supernatural beings, so it is not surprising to see so many new shows popping up regarding all types of magical and mystical creatures. I love these kinds of shows, however, after watching such delightful entertainment as *Being Human* (2010/2011), I don't think I could handle the life of a werewolf—I enjoy my meat cooked medium well.

PART TWO

MAGICK

"The werewolves are certayne sorcerers, who having annoynted their bodies with an oyntment which they make by the instinct of the devil, and putting on a certayne inchaunted girdle, doe not onely unto the view of others seeme as wolves, but to their owne thinking have both the shape and nature of wolves, so long as they weare the said girdle. And they do dispose themselves as very wolves, in wourrying and killing, and most of humane creatures."

~ Richard Verstegan

Restitution of Decayed Intelligence, 1628

TRANSFORMATION MAGICK

"Were such things here as we do speak about?
Or have we eaten on the insane root
That takes the reason prisoner?"

~Shakespeare
Macbeth I.iii

These old rituals and spells are passed down from our ancestors of the past.

Please understand the words are not to be taken lightly and some of these ingredients are

EXTREMELY DEADLY.

The publisher and author will not be held responsible for the actions you, the reader, may take.

I say this all the time when it comes to rituals, recipes, and spells from those occultists and magus long ago... Rarely did they include reversals, so what you do, you do at your own risk.

TURN SOMEONE INTO A BEAR

This is done by dissolving or boiling the brains and heart of that animal in new wine, and then giving it to anyone to drink out of the skull. While the force of the draught operates he/she will fancy every living creature to be a bear like to himself; neither can anything divert or cure him until the fumes and virtue of the liquor are entirely expended, no other distemper being perceivable in him.

TO TRANSFORM INTO A CROW

With this transformation spell, write these letters on virgin parchment. Make sure to get the real virgin parchment paper, which is made from the skin/belly of a sheep. The paper is extremely hard to find, but a few occult or magical suppliers have or can find the paper for you. With each letter written, concentrate on an image of a crow.

R O L O R
O B U F O
L U A U L
O F U B O
R O L O R

FAMOUS FLYING/WEREWOLF OINTMENT

These are the famous ingredients, for those who wish to experience flight in motion or supposedly feel, or become a werewolf. Remember that most of these ingredients are **very toxic and could seriously harm or even cause death.** Here is a list of ingredients used but also includes the extras that were once added to the ointment as well. This ointment was either rubbed sometimes in-between the thighs or even inhaled at times.

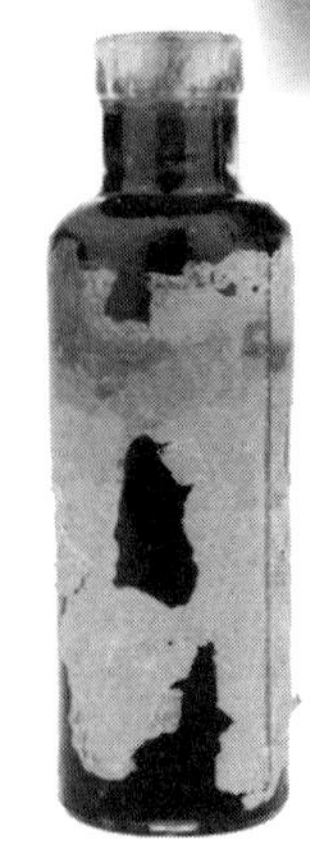

Belladonna
Henbane
Hemlock
Wolfsbane
Opium (sometimes just the seeds crushed)
Cinquefoil
Aconite
Mandrake
Parsley
Foxglove
Semen
Bat's Blood or Cat's (black)
Urine
Baby fat (taken from unbaptized babies who are deceased)
Or dog, wolf fat
Menstrual blood
Cat bone (crushed into powder)
Toad excrements

Whilst researching the formula for werewolf ointment I came across an old text which describes in some detail exactly how to go about working the necessary magick to change into a werewolf. This did involve summoning spirits to assist in the change. I do not encourage anyone to attempt this feat due to the fact (as I mentioned) that most of these spells have no real reversals!

> The locality chosen, our candidate must next select a night when the moon is new and strong. He must then choose a perfectly level piece of ground, and on it, at midnight, he must mark, either with chalk or string—it really does not matter which—a circle of not less than seven feet in radius, and within this, and from the same centre, another circle of three feet in radius. Then, in the centre of this inner circle he must kindle a fire, and over the fire place an iron tripod containing an iron vessel of water. As soon as the water begins to boil the would-be lycanthropist must throw into it handfuls of any three of the following substances: Asafœtida, parsley,

opium, hemlock, henbane, saffron, aloe, poppy-seed and solanum; repeating as he does so these words:

"Spirits from the deep
Who never sleep,
Be kind to me.

"Spirits from the grave
Without a soul to save,
Be kind to me.

"Spirits of the trees
That grow upon the leas,
Be kind to me.

"Spirits of the air,
Foul and black, not fair,
Be kind to me.

"Water spirits hateful,
To ships and bathers fateful,
Be kind to me.

"Spirits of earthbound dead
That glide with noiseless tread,
Be kind to me.

"Spirits of heat and fire,
Destructive in your ire,
Be kind to me.

"Spirits of cold and ice,
Patrons of crime and vice,
Be kind to me.

"Wolves, vampires, satyrs, ghosts!
Elect of all the devilish hosts!
I pray you send hither,
Send hither, send hither,
The great grey shape that makes men shiver!
Shiver, shiver, shiver!
Come! Come! Come!"

> The supplicant then takes off his vest and shirt and smears his body with the fat of some newly killed animal (preferably a cat), mixed with aniseed, camphor, and opium. Then he binds round his loins a girdle made of wolf's-skin, and kneeling down within the circumference of the first circle, waits for the advent of the Unknown. When the fire burns blue and quickly dies out, the Unknown is about to manifest itself; if it does not actually appear, it will make its presence felt.
>
> There is little consistency in the various methods of the spirit's advent: Sometimes a deep unnatural silence immediately precedes it; sometimes crashes and bangs, groanings and shriekings, herald its approach. When it remains invisible, its presence is indicated and accompanied by a sensation of abnormal cold and the most acute terror. It is sometimes visible in the guise of a huntsman—which is, perhaps, its most popular shape—sometimes in the form of a monstrosity, partly man and partly beast—and sometimes it is seen ill defined and only partially materialized. To what order of spirits it belongs is, of course, purely a matter of conjecture. I believe it to be some malevolent, super physical, creative power, such as, in my opinion, participated largely in the creation of this and other planets. I do not believe it to be the Devil, because I do not believe in the existence of only one devil, but in countless devils. It is difficult to say to what extent the Unknown is believed to be powerful by those who approach it for the purpose of acquiring the gift of lycanthropy; but I am inclined to think that the majority of these, at all events, do not ascribe to it any supreme power, but regard it merely as a local spirit—the spirit of some particular wilderness or forest.

I'm not quite certain as to where Mr. O'Donnell the author of the text *Werewolves* got his spells from, as he repeatedly refers to those who talk to him as "informants." However, I find the above spell very interesting and can definitely see a link between this and the werewolf or witch's flying ointment used during the medieval periods of European history.

RUSSIAN SPELL TO TURN INTO A WOLF

Many people get confused as there are three names for the werewolf in Russian but each name signifies a different way that they changed. The first one is vlkodlak which signified someone who was cursed, the second is wawkalak, common among white Russians. This term refers to someone who has been punished by the devil. Lastly, we have the oborot which means "one transformed" and signifies someone who freely instituted the change through their own will. The following is a spell to transform oneself willingly into the form of a wolf.

> He who desires to become an oborot, let him seek in the forest a hewn-down tree; let him stab it with a small copper knife, and walk round the tree, repeating the following incantation:
>
> On the sea, on the ocean, on the island, on Bujan,
> On the empty pasture gleams
> the moon, on an ashstock lying
> In a green wood, in a gloomy vale.
> Toward the stock wandereth a shaggy wolf.
> Horned cattle seeking for his sharp white fangs;
> But the wolf enters not the forest,
> But the wolf dives not into the shadowy vale,
> Moon, moon, gold-horned moon,
> Cheek the flight of bullets, blunt the hunters' knives,
> Break the shepherds' cudgels,
> Cast wild fear upon all cattle,
> On men, on all creeping things,
> That they may not catch the grey wolf,
> That they may not rend his warm skin
> My word is binding, more binding than sleep,
> More binding than the promise of a hero!
>
> "Then he springs thrice over the tree and runs into the forest, transformed into a wolf.

13 MORE WAYS TO BECOME A WERE-BEAST

Most of what I will be citing now comes from folklore and legends.

1. Create a belt from the skin of a wolf that has just been killed, gather the skin before the body gets cold signifying that the spirit has left. Wrap the belt three times around your body and get ready for the change. The same has also been done with foxes.

2. Drink from a pond or stream in which three wolves recently shared a drink.

3. Be born on a New Moon.

4. Drink water from the footprint of a wolf.

5. Eat the brains or flesh of a wolf.

6. Commit sacrilege.

7. Inherit it (It's hereditary).

8. Be born on Christmas Day.

9. Wear an animal skin (of your choice, but keep in mind that is what you will turn into... No skunks please!) Or wear a jacket with the fur still attached.

10. Wear or eat the flower known as Lycanthropus found in the Balkan Peninsula; it comes in the colors of white and yellow. The smell is reminiscent of death and it exudes a sticky white sap.

11. Eat the meat of an animal that a wolf recently killed.

12. Survive an attack from a werewolf.

13. Have the saliva of a werewolf spread on you.

Again, this is one of those things where if I were to list every possible spell, enchantment and ritual, well...the book would be gigantic, so these are some of my personal favorites, both popular and rare.

REVERSE THE CURSE

SIGNS AND SAVINGS

If you have a friend who you believe may be a werewolf, there are some signs to watch for. The Russians believed that if you looked beneath the tongue while the potential werewolf was in human form, there would be bristles.

If a person has a love of raw meat and refuses other foods, develops a uni-brow, or their eyes go flat and dull... well, they might just be a shapeshifter.

But how do you save a friend or yourself from a permanent change?

A BELGIAN EXORCISM RECIPE

A werewolf is sprinkled with a compound of either 1/2 ounce of sulphur, 4 drachms of asafoetida, 1/4 ounce of castoreum; or of 3/4 ounce of hypericum in 3 ounces of vinegar; or with a solution of carbolic acid further diluted with a pint of clear spring water. The sprinkling must be done over the head and shoulders, and the werewolf must at the same time be addressed in his Christian name.

THE SILVER BULLET

From Stephen King's movie to Van Helsing, silver bullets have been used for hundreds of years to kill werewolves... or have they? It is believed that folklorists actually added the silver bullet, but who is to say it does not work. I have not killed any werewolves lately...so I really don't know. That being said, it is a little extreme to kill your friend. There are plenty of other methods but this one guarantees that they will change back to their human shape...in death.

IRON & STEEL

This will not break the spell, curse, or enchantment, but will change them back for a time. Throw a piece of iron or steel over the werewolf's head. If this would work for a short while, maybe finding a way to attach said piece to the wolf would keep the change permanently?

FIND THEIR CLOTHES

In some legends it is said that in order for a were-beast to change back permanently, especially if changing at will, they must find their clothes by sunup, otherwise they will remain in their animal form forever.

DO IT BACKWARDS

Whatever spell has been created (such as that of jumping over a stump) the shapeshifter must do it backwards in order to bring them back to human form.

CALL THEIR NAME

In many of the legends, especially those citing the use of the wolf or fox belt, if you call the werewolf by their baptized Christian name three times, then they will turn back.

WOUND IT

Unfortunately, sometimes these shapeshifters have to endure a little pain in order to change back into their human form. You don't have to kill your friend, but in an intense reaction to pain (such as by stabbing them in the leg or arm), they will change back into their human self.

BE A VAMPIRE

Draw three drops of the blood while the shapeshifter is in werewolf form.

BUMP ON THE HEAD

Hit the werewolf three times on the head with a knife. I'm not particularly sure which end, but if it's a friend I would try the blunt end first.

These are just some of the many different ways to help a friend or yourself turn back into your human form. Throughout many of the legends, it has been up to humans to save the werewolf. So if you are a physical shapeshifter and you are stuck, find a friend who will understand and point them to this book.

PART THREE

MYSTERY

"I think we all have to fight the werewolf within us somehow."

~Will Kemp

ILLNESS AND DISEASE

HYPERTRICHOSIS

Human Werewolf Syndrome, does seem to sounds like something right out of a science fiction movie. However, this is in fact a true medical condition also known as Hypertrichosis—a condition, that causes abnormal amounts of hair to grow on a person's body. This can happen while still in the mother's womb or even later in the individual's life. For children born with this condition, the lanugo, which is hair that covers the entire body, has not shed. The hair is supposed to fall off at around 33 to 36 weeks of pregnancy to be replaced by vellus hair. With Hypertrichosis in children, the lanugo actually changes from a fine hair almost white or transparent hair to one of color; the strands harden into thickness and texture similar to the hair on your head. Sometimes a baby can be born with a small patch or patches of lanugo, which will fall off. Most commonly it is seen on the shoulders. I can remember standing in the checkout line at the supermarket, and glancing over at the tabloid magazines. There on the front cover was a picture of a young boy covered head to toe in what seemed to look like fur. Of course, the tabloid did not mention a word about medical circumstance and portrayed the child as a "werewolf" offspring.

LIONEL, THE LION-FACED MAN

Stephan Bibrowski was an excellent example of hypertrichosis at its finest.

Throughout his life in the sideshow, Lionel maintained respect and dignity always acting the gentleman. He may have been one of the best-educated side-show entertainers around multilingual and taught at a Catholic school in his early days.

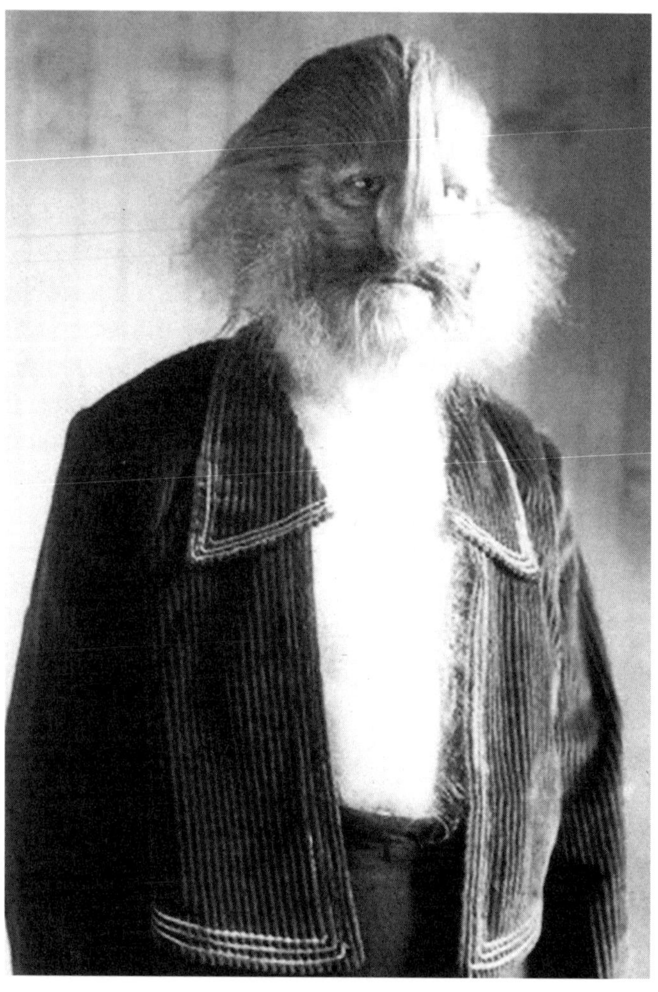

Stephan Bibrowski when he first arrived in the USA via Ellis Island, New York.

There are two separate accounts of his childhood before hooking up with the traveling band of all things weird. Both accounts say that his mother watched his father get mauled by a lion whist she was pregnant and that he was originally from Poland. However, one account portrays her as a loving woman who wanted only to care for her children, even with the condition that Stephan (later to be Lionel) had, but that it was the small rural community that she lived in that forced her to give away her son and move. Others say that when she saw her son right after birth already covered in hair, she thought him to be an abomination and handed him over to the impresario name Meyer.

Personally, I like to believe the first account. Either way, Lionel went on to become a world famous attraction. He came to the United States multiple times and eventually became a citizen of Germany. At one point he was also contracted by Barnum and Bailey. Always photographed in a relaxed pose, dressed to the nines, and carrying a book, his soft voice and courteous demeanor was the exact opposite of what everyone expected him to be. People went in assuming he would be a ferocious beast and all they would find is this smart thinking man who just had some extra body hair.

'ATES IMMIGRATION OFFICER AT PORT OF ARRIVAL

List 6

The entries on this sheet must be typewritten or printed.

...r a part of another insular possession, in whatsoever class they travel, MUST be fully listed and the master or commanding officer of each vessel carrying such passengers must upon arrival deliver lists thereof to the immigration officer.
...D-CABIN PASSENGERS ONLY

...iving at Port of NEW YORK, 19 99

16 By whom was passage paid?	17	18 Whether ever before in the United States	19 Whether going to join a relative or friend; and if so, what relative or friend, and his name and complete address	20			21	22–23	24	25	26	27 Condition of health, mental and physical	28 Deformed or crippled	29 Height	30 Complexion	31 Color of Hair	Eyes	32 Marks of identification	33 Place of birth: Country	City or town
DAUGHTER	25	NO	DAUGHTER:JRA SPARROW WHITE LAKE,D.DAKOTA	NO	PERMAN	YES	NO	NONO	NO	NO	NO	GOOD	NO	5 7	FAIR	BL	GR	NONE	GERMANY	[illegible]BORN
SISTER	25	NO	SISTER: AS ABOVE	NO	DO	YES	NO	NONO	NO	NO	NO	GOOD	NO	5 9	FAIR	BR	BR	3rd & 4th FINGER L.HAND CRIPPLED.	DO	WIESBADEN
MOTHER	-	NO	MOTHER: AS ABOVE	NO	DO	YES	NO	NONO	NO	NO	NO	GOOD	NO	- -	FAIR	BR	BL	NONE	DO	DO
EMPLOYER	YES	NO	ACQ: S.W.GUMPERTZ, DREAMLAND CIRCUS SIDE SHOW CONEY ISLAND NY	Y	6 MONTH	NO	NO	NONO	NO	NO	NO	GOOD	NO	5 7	FAIR	GR	BR	NONE	DO	ESSEN
EMPLOYER	YES	NO	ACQ: AS ABOVE	YES	6 MONTH	NO	NO	NONO	NO	NO	NO	GOOD	NO	5 7	FAIR	BL	BR	NONE	DO	HAVN
EMPLOYER	YES	NO	ACQ: AS ABOVE	YES	6 MONTH	NO	NO	NONO	NO	NO	NO	GOOD	NO	5 5	FAIR	[illegible]	[illegible]	THE WHOLE BODY COVERED WITH HAIRS.	POLAND	[illegible]GRAGOVA
SELF	25	NO	BROTHER: GEORG HEIGL, 1290 NEWPORT AVE, NORTHAMPTON PA.	NO	PERMAN	Y	NO	NONO	NO	NO	NO	GOOD	NO	5 9	FAIR	BR	BR	CRIPPLED LEFT INDEX FINGER	AUSTRIA	KIRCHFIDISCH
BR 1/1	25	NO	BROTHER 1/1: ARNOLD KLEINRATH 1641 N.HALSTEDSTR CHICAGO ILL	NO	DO	YES	NO	NONO	NO	NO	NO	GOOD	NO	[illegible]	[illegible]	[illegible]	[illegible]	[illegible]	[illegible]	[illegible]

Stephan Bibrowski's US Immigration Entry. Under the description it says, "The whole body covered in hair." Ellis Island 1923.

Around the age of 40, Lionel finally retired. Unfortunately, after his retirement his life is undocumented so there is not much known. Some say he died of a heart attack in 1931; others assert that he passed in 1932. Either way, Lionel was a fabulous man with much to offer the world.

HIRSUTISM AND THE BEARDED LADY

Hirsutism comes from the Latin *hirsutus* meaning "rough, shaggy" and *isme* a suffix used to denote a condition, state, or doctrine. Nowadays, it is seen not as an illness, but a condition. However, in the times of the pagans, even the Goddesses had beards. Aphrodite hailed as the most beautiful of the pantheon, looked to for love, and caretaker of women...had a beard. However, that image is no longer as prominent as those of her in beautiful flowing skirts with long hair. In the book *Saturnalia,* there is a nice description of a statue of Aphrodite (therein named as Aphrodito) in Cyprus with a beard. False beards would also be associated with women of Ancient Egypt where beards were looked down upon by the common person as they were symbols of the Gods.

A woman with hirsutism as depicted in Nuremberg Chronicle 1493.

So tightly braided, they shone like lapis lazuli, however, Kings and Queens would wear false beards for portraiture such as Queen Hatshepsut.

In pagan times, women who naturally grew beards were considered to be of both sexes, and they were attributed as having supernatural powers, close to those of the gods. As Christianity became the dominant religion, people's outlook on the beard changed; it turned into a stigma. A woman with a beard was someone to stay away from. They could wreak havoc and bring bad crops; they might have even had associations with the devil.

In William Shakespeare's *Macbeth,* it clearly outlines this new thought process regarding witches when Banquo is not quite sure how to address the three bearded ones.

> How far is't call'd to Forres? What are these So wither'd and so wild in their attire, That look not like the inhabitants o' the earth, And yet are on't? Live you? Or are you aught That man may question? You seem to understand me, By each at once her chappy finger laying Upon her skinny lips: you should be women, And yet your beards forbid me to interpret That you are so.

HOW HIRSUTISM WORKS

Many believe this condition results only in bearded ladies, but that is not the case. Some grow hair on their backs, chests, or shoulders. Hirsutism is caused by an overabundance of the male hormone androgen. This condition does not usually show until the start of puberty when girls begin to go through their hormonal changes.

There are many different causes of Hirsutism; here are just a few:

- Polycystic ovarian syndrome (PCOS)—may also cause infertility
- Tumors on the adrenal glands or ovaries
- Cushing syndrome
- Medications that can cause hair growth—phenytoin, minoxidil, diazoxide, cyclosporine, and hexachlorobenzene
- Anabolic steroids
- Danazol—used to treat endometriosis
- Obesity

Typically, if the condition is natural, the hair is long and fine whereas if it is caused by injecting hormone, it is more coarse, larger and darker, following the pattern of men's hair. Due to the fact that they have found hirsutism to be connected with many ovarian issues, if you feel you have hirsutism, do not be surprised if your doctors asks about your menstrual cycle. They also assess the patient by physicality and male traits aside from just the hair. Adrenal glands that help to secrete the hormones may also be tested to make sure there is nothing else going on. Birth control pills have helped one in ten sufferers and spironolactone, which is prescribed to slow hair growth, has helped seventy percent of the people it was prescribed to. Together, they can help to regulate the menstrual cycle if that is an issue and slow down the hair growth to almost nil.

P.T. BARNUM'S BEARDED LADY

"Come one, come all!
Meet the Bearded Lady!"

Annie Jones was born in Virginia on July 14th supposedly with a full scruff of beard on her chin. Her parents, both normal looking, were horrified at their little daughter.

Annie Jones "Infant of Esau" had hirsutism 1881-1895.

Eventually, they came to recognize a financial opportunity and they gave her over to P.T. Barnum, Connecticut native and showman extraordinaire. Annie was then peddled around as the "Infant of Esau," a reference to the biblical name Esau, son of Abraham, brother of Jacob. In traditional Hebrew it meant "hairy." During the Victorian Era with such prudence and stringent rules, the sideshow was one place where Victorians could look upon imperfection and enjoy it, or hassle it.

At 9 months, it is said that Annie was already performing as part of Barnum's second American Museum and that when it was burned down, she was stolen and shopped around privately throughout Europe until 1867. The thief was arrested in Canada and Annie was returned to her parents.

After the burning, Barnum was about ready to give up he was almost sixty, old by the day's standards, as he had been in business almost thirty years. Then friend C.C. Wallace came to him two years after the burning and "convinced" him (I use that term loosely because I can't imagine it took much) to start a traveling museum, menagerie, and circus.

> A bearded girl has made her appearance at Glade Springs Depot, Washington County, VA. She is four years old, and has a moustache and whiskers, the hair upon the forehead extending to the eyebrows. Very heavy hair, exceedingly black, extends below the shoulders. The child is sprightly, with fully developed limbs and well-formed body. The arms, shoulders and back are covered with soft, downy hair.
>
> ~News clipping 1870

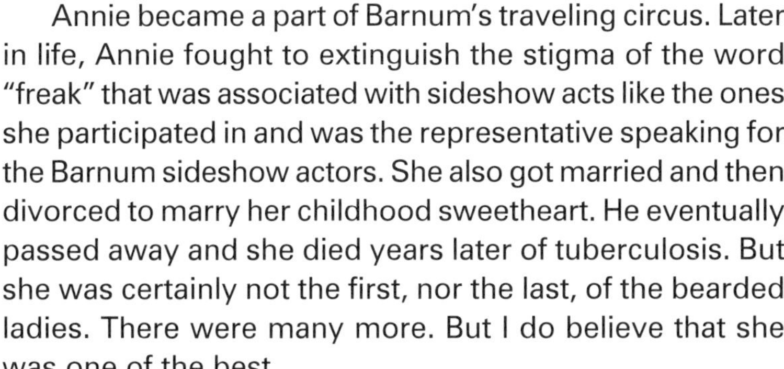

Annie became a part of Barnum's traveling circus. Later in life, Annie fought to extinguish the stigma of the word "freak" that was associated with sideshow acts like the ones she participated in and was the representative speaking for the Barnum sideshow actors. She also got married and then divorced to marry her childhood sweetheart. He eventually passed away and she died years later of tuberculosis. But she was certainly not the first, nor the last, of the bearded ladies. There were many more. But I do believe that she was one of the best.

CLINICAL LYCANTHROPY

Lycanthropy is no longer the word to use for werewolves, ever since it became a medical term.

Just what is Clinical Lycanthropy? It is a delusion of the mind commonly associated or accompanied by other medical conditions such as schizophrenia, psychotic disorders, and clinical depression. A patient suffering from this psychological disorder will most assuredly assert the belief that he/she is in fact either a wolf-like creature or can shapeshift into such form of one.

The other side of it is as a way of depersonalization when dealing with hardships and depression. In other words, this person is creating an alternate "person," or animal in this case, to protect him or herself. The only real difference between this and dissociative identity disorder is that the person knows about it. There was a case study printed about the connections between clinical lycanthropy and depression in the *Iranian Medicine*. It clearly shows how clinical lycanthropy can sometimes be a symptom of a much larger problem.

Case Report

In the journal scientists featured a twenty year old laborer who had a stutter since he was twelve years old. He did not contact the doctors, but was instead referred to them as he had been complaining of turning into a wolf for the past two months. His symptoms were varied: He felt that he had unlimited strength even when in human form, he would attack others, at times he felt so connected to the wolf-self that he would walk on all fours. Most often these feelings and delusions would come to pass during times of loneliness and he would stay in this state anywhere from one to three hours. When it was over, the patient would be extremely confused and anxious; at times he would also have a headache or light-headedness.

Cannabalism in 1557 as told by Hans Staden.

> He was not the only one to suffer from this wolf spirit. The patient believed that at times, others around him also transformed. They sometimes became wolves; others became leopards—whatever they shifted into they were always trying to kill him. Aside from the shapeshifting, he had a multitude of other delusions, such as bugs crawling in his body, hypnagogic hallucinations (visions that occur upon waking), and foul odors. Born in a highly religious family, the patient never really knew how to adjust to school and life within his society.
>
> The scientists ran him through a battery of tests—everything from CT scans to IQ tests, which all came back normal. Eventually, they diagnosed him with delusional depression based on interviews with family, the patient, and the feedback from the tests. He was treated with anti-psychotic and anti-depressants. Over the two years of treatment, the symptoms of the lycanthropy and depression declined.

Other cases of clinical lycanthropy have shown the sufferers to have extremely disturbing sexual behavior, such as one woman who in the midst of a family barbecue stripped completely naked and began running around on all fours, eventually asking her mother (whilst on all fours) to have sex with her. But according to P.E. Keck in his article *Lycanthropy: Alive and Well in the Twentieth Century,* he asserts that the delusions that the patient suffers from may not be completely under their control. It is also believed that the presence of lycanthropy should not affect the outcome of any earlier detected disease or psychological issue. In this case, the doctors saw this and treated it as one problem and it worked. After two years, the signs of depression were still there but the signs of lycanthropy had decreased immensely. Clinical lycanthropy, whether a part of another illness puzzle or on its own, is a disturbing psychological phenomena, one that is dangerous and not to be taken lightly.

RABIES

Violent outburst, insomnia, abnormal behavior, and hallucinations are a few of the symptoms of the virus called rabies. If left untreated, rabies will attack the brain and central nervous system. If not caught within the first twenty-four to forty-eight hours, the victim has a high likelihood of suffering a slow and painful death. Imagine such a painful and terrifying experience for the victim to endure on any level. Rabies is not an airborne virus, but rather a virus that spreads through a scratch, bite, and saliva. In almost all cases, the symptoms do not appear until at least a few weeks to several months after the attack depending on how quickly the virus spreads to the nervous system, and that means it's far too late for most any type of cure. No wonder our ancestors thought there were those demon-possessed individuals and werewolves running around the villages attacking people. Without the proper medical knowledge during those times, of course fear was pulsing through the veins of the villagers.

If a person is bitten and hopefully contacts their doctor and State Health Department right away, a post-exposure shot called "human rabies immunoglobulin" or known as post exposure prophylaxis (PEP) will be given within twenty-four to forty-eight hours of the attack.

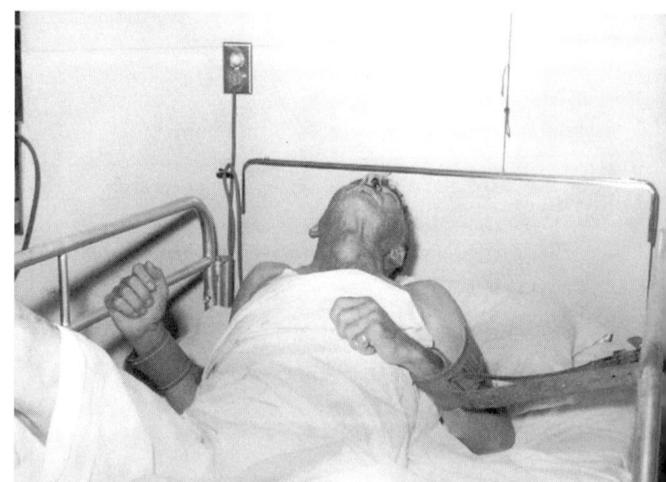

A patient with rabies 1959.

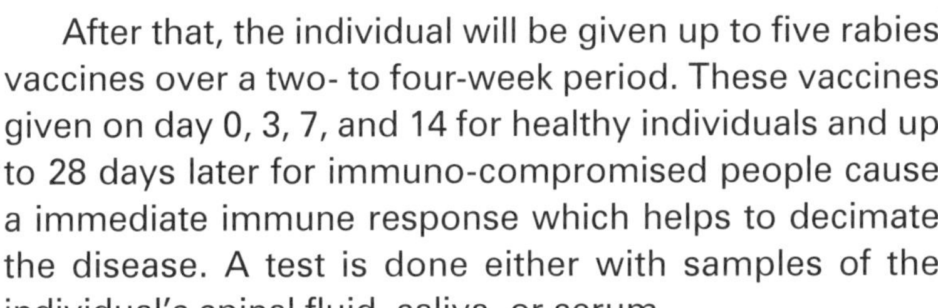

After that, the individual will be given up to five rabies vaccines over a two- to four-week period. These vaccines given on day 0, 3, 7, and 14 for healthy individuals and up to 28 days later for immuno-compromised people cause a immediate immune response which helps to decimate the disease. A test is done either with samples of the individual's spinal fluid, saliva, or serum.

The times have changed with how the injections are given; years ago, it was a long syringe needle inserted into the stomach area—not a pleasant experience to say the least. Today, such injections are given right into the arm's tissue with a much smaller needle. But what if the animal is not acting strangely or extremely violent, and an individual does get bitten and shrugs the incident off? A very bad move, but I am sure it does and will happen. What if the animal did in fact have rabies though it was not at the noticeable stage yet? Early symptoms are fever, weakness, seizures, headaches, and itching sensations around the bite or scratch area. (Itching of the bite area? I'm having a flashback to almost every werewolf movie I've ever seen... Are you?) As time passes, the pain and symptoms get much worse.

Each year, around the world, approximately 40,000 to 50,000 individuals die from rabies because there is little or no supply of the vaccines. The United States death rate due to the virus is minimal because of the high availability of the vaccine. So then I have to wonder, why aren't the countries banding together to fight this virus and save the lives of thousands of people?

Testing on suspected animals is common; the test is called direct fluorescent antibody. Unfortunately, it is not a blood test where the animal can be freed afterward, because rabies is carried in the central nervous system and the brain. The virus would not show up in a simple blood smear. To find out whether an animal is truly a carrier, they have to test the brain tissues, thusly sacrificing the animal whether innocent or guilty. It is a preventative and one that must be taken.

REAL-LIFE FLESH EATERS

WARNING: The information in this chapter contains gruesome details from cases of those individuals who have mauled, murdered, and eaten parts or all of their victims.

There are real-life monsters which each of us in the world at one time or another has walked or passed by in our travels and never knew it. For a brief moment, we find ourselves standing in the presence of a real flesh-eating monster. Would we take notice when a stranger says hello on the street or in a store, watching our every move? Could an innocent person who is going about daily life be a next victim or even worse, a next meal? It has definitely happened throughout our history and is still happing today; no one is immune. No one!

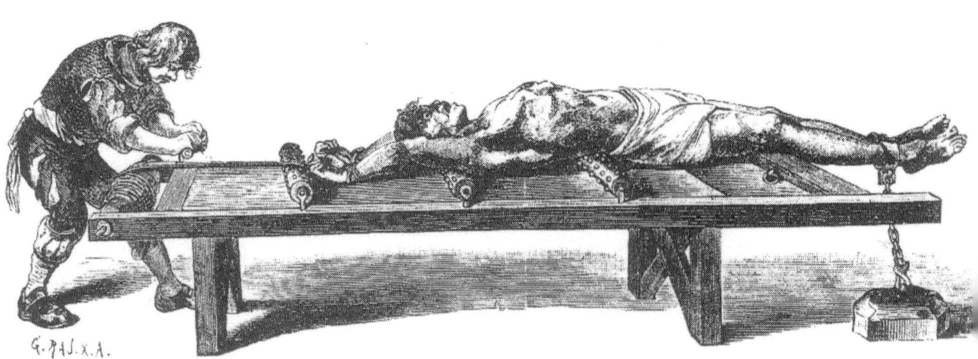

Medieval torture rack.

THE WEREWOLF OF DOLE, FRANCE
GILLES GARNIER

On November 8, 1573, a group of villagers were coming home from finishing some work in the woods. As they walked, suddenly, they heard the screams of a little girl and the howling of a monster. Running in the direction of the sound, they came upon a little girl who looked like she was being attacked by a loup garou that was bent over her scratching and biting. As they approached, it ran away on all fours into the brush nearby. It was too dark to tell exactly what it was; no one was sure if it was a beast or a man. This incident was followed with that of a boy who suddenly disappeared about a week later. Three more children after that succumbed to the abominable beast's attacks.

Over the next month or so, the villagers continued to fall victim and eventually the loup-garou went after adults. Talk amongst the town folk became more heated and fingers began to be pointed. They started to talk about the hermit, Gilles. On December 3, 1573, the authorities gave the villagers permission to hunt the monster. The following is the decree:

> According to the advertisement made to the sovereign Court of the Parliament at Dole, that, in the territories of Espagny, Salvange, Courchapon, and the neighboring villages, has often been seen and met, for some time past, a werewolf, who, it is said, has already seized and carried off several little children, so that they have not been seen since, and since he had attacked and done injury in the country to some horsemen, who kept him off only with great difficulty and danger to their persons: the said Court, desiring to prevent any greater danger, has permitted, and does permit, those who are abiding or dwelling in the said places and others, notwithstanding all edicts concerning the chase [i.e., a ban on hunting] to assemble with pikes, halberts,

> arquebuses, and sticks, to chase and to pursue the said werewolf in every place where they may find or seize him; to tie and to kill, without incurring any pains or penalties.

The villagers caught Gilles Garnier while attacking one of his victims. Capturing him while he was still in his wolf form, he was recognized by the townspeople as the murderer. Garnier was said to be a:

> ...somber, ill-looking fellow, who walked in a stooping attitude, and whose pale face, livid complexion, and deep-set eyes under a pair of coarse and bushy eyebrows, which met across the forehead [one of the signs of werewolfism], were sufficient to repel any one from seeking his acquaintance. Gilles seldom spoke, and when he did it was in the broadest patois [vernacular] of his country. His long gray beard and retiring habits procured him the name the Hermit of St. Bonnot, though no one for a moment attributed to him any extraordinary amount of sanctity.

During his interrogation he admitted to killing many people one being a little girl who he ripped apart with his teeth and claws eating some of her and taking the rest home to his wife.

In another recorded account given to Henry Camus, he said this:

> ...was to the effect that he, Gilles Garnier, had seized upon a little girl, twelve years of age, whom he drew into a vineyard and there killed, partly with his teeth and partly with his hands, seeming like wolf's paws; that from thence he trailed her bleeding body along the ground with his teeth into the wood of La Serre, where he ate the greatest portion of her at one meal, and carried the remainder home to his wife; that upon another occasion, eight days before the festival of All

> Saints, he was seen to seize another child in his teeth, and would have devoured her had she not been rescued by the country people, and that the said child died a few days afterwards of the injuries he had inflicted; that fifteen days after the same festival of All Saints, being again in the shape of a wolf, he devoured a boy thirteen years of age, having previously torn off his leg and thigh with his teeth, and hid them away for his breakfast on the morrow. He was furthermore indicted for giving way to the same diabolical and unnatural propensities even in his shape of a man, and that he had strangled a boy in a wood with the intention of eating him, which crime he would have effected if he had not been seen by the neighbors and prevented.

Altogether, over fifty people testified at his trial, detailing the horrors that this monster inflicted upon the town. Ultimately, Gilles was put to the rack upon which he confessed to his every crime and was then beheaded on January 8, 1574, effectively ending the wrath of the loup-garou's reign of terror.

THE CASE OF PETER STUBBE

Even though this case is very well known to most individuals who have read about the subject of werewolves, cannibals, and murderers, how could I not write about the infamous case of Peter Stubbe? He was also known as Peter Stumpp, Peter Stube, Peter Stumf and Peter Stübbe. The most famous name that Peter was given throughout history was the "Werewolf of Bedburg." Now it gets a bit confusing because Peter is known, too, as Abal Griswold, Abil Griswold, and Ubel Griswold. Supposedly, or rumor has it, that Peter was nick named "Stubbe" due to the loss of one hand, though we are not sure exactly how the hand was removed because there is no other mention of the incident in the history of the story.

Lucas Cranach the Elder.

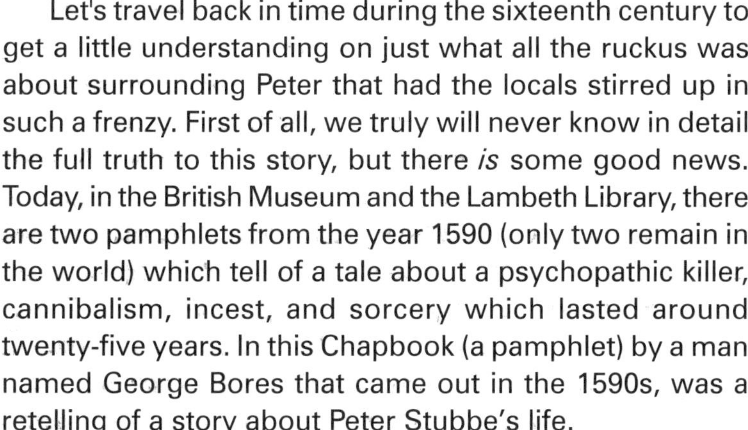

Let's travel back in time during the sixteenth century to get a little understanding on just what all the ruckus was about surrounding Peter that had the locals stirred up in such a frenzy. First of all, we truly will never know in detail the full truth to this story, but there *is* some good news. Today, in the British Museum and the Lambeth Library, there are two pamphlets from the year 1590 (only two remain in the world) which tell of a tale about a psychopathic killer, cannibalism, incest, and sorcery which lasted around twenty-five years. In this Chapbook (a pamphlet) by a man named George Bores that came out in the 1590s, was a retelling of a story about Peter Stubbe's life.

> In the towns of Cperadt and Bedbur near Collin in high Germany, there was continually brought up and nourished one Stubbe Peeter, who from his youth was greatly inclined to evil and the practicing of wicked arts even from twelve years of age till twenty, and so forwards till his dying day, insomuch that surfeiting in the damnable desire of magic, necromancy, and sorcery, acquainting himself with many infernal spirits and fiends, insomuch that forgetting the God that made him, and that Savior that shed his blood man man's redemption: In the end, careless of salvation gave both soul and body to the Devil forever, for small carnal pleasure in this life, that he might be famous and spoken of on earth, though he lost heaven thereby.

Now, most of us know the history, or should know, of the horrific burning times or witch/werewolf trials. When during the fourteenth to the seventeenth century between 50,000 and 60,000 individuals were executed. I am sure the head count is much larger but not recorded or written down for history. No one was safe, not even your child or beloved house pet. Absolutely, there were many, and I mean many, individuals who in fact were innocent, yet that word meant nothing during these horrific slaughtering times. But was Peter a "real" werewolf?

The breaking wheel was used during the Middle Ages and was in use into the nineteenth century.

Supposedly, the story is that one day some local hunters went off into the woods to hunt down this evil creature who was believed to have viscously murdering almost eighteen individuals by ripping the flesh right off their bodies and eating the raw meat. Livestock was brutally attacked; children and young women were found in a bloody scene all in pieces. Among the victims was Peter's young son, found torn apart and his head smashed in with parts of his brain eaten away. It was rumored around the town that Peter's son was born by the act of incest with his own daughter named Beel. George Bores writes on this act of incest between Peter and his daughter:

> He had at that time living a fair young damsel to his daughter, after whom he also lusted most unnaturally, and cruelly committed most wicked incest with her, a most gross and vile sin, far surmounting adultery or fornication, though the least of the three doth drive the soul into hell fire, except hearty repentance, and the great mercy of God. This daughter of his he begot when he was not altogether so wickedly given, who was called by the name of Stubbe Beell, whose beauty and good grace was such as deserved commendations of all those that knew her. And such was his inordinate lust and filthy desire toward her, that he begat a child by her, daily using her as his concubine; but as an insatiate and filthy beast, given over to work evil, with greediness he also lay by his own sister, frequenting her company long time, even according as the wickedness of his heart led him.

All right, as the hunters were still searching for this unholy of a monster deep in the woods, they followed a bloody trail from a young woman who was brutally attacked, her stomach's insides ripped out, along with her unborn child. Such fear and panic struck the faces of the men, until they caught sight of something or someone, off in the distance.

Again, George Bores sets the best scene for us.

> And, although they had practiced all the means that men could devise to take this ravenous beast, yet until the Lord had determined his fall, they could not in any wise prevail: notwithstanding, they daily continued their purpose, and daily sought to entrap him, and for that intent continually maintained great mastiffs and dogs of much strength to hunt and chase the beast. In the end, it pleased God, as they were in readiness and provided to meet with him, that they should spy him in his wolfish likeness at what time they beset him round about, and most circumspectly set their dogs upon

> him, in such sort that there was no means of escape, at which advantage they never could get him before; but as the Lord delivered Goliath into the hands of David, so was this wolf brought in danger of these men, who seeing, as I said before, no way to escape the imminent danger, being hardly pursued at the heels, presently slipped his girdle from about him, whereby the shape of a wolf clean avoided, and he appeared presently in his true shape and likeness, having in his hand a staff as one walking toward the city. But the hunters, whose eyes were steadfastly bent upon the beast, and seeing him in the same place metamorphosed contrary to their expectation, it wrought a wonderful amazement to their minds; and, had it not been that they knew the man so soon as they saw him, they had surely taken the same to have been some Devil in a man's likeness; but for as much as they knew him to be an ancient dweller in the town, they came unto him, and talking with him, they brought him by communication home to his own house, and finding him to be the man indeed, and no delusion or fantastical motion, they had him incontinent before the magistrates to be examined.

Peter's fate was now in the hands of his peers and jury, but while under questioning per court style back during the ages; the famous "rack" played a key role into the questions and answers. Peter confessed about being a werewolf and a sorcerer since his early teens. He spoke of a magical belt given to him by Satan himself which could turn him into a wolf/werewolf once the belt was placed on his waist. Of course, we must remember that Peter was getting his body stretched which causes the bones to dislocate, not a pleasurable feeling. Most tortured victims said anything to please the questioner in order to stop the pain. Peter was no different. While a group of men ventured off in search of this magical belt for proof of Peter's story, each man

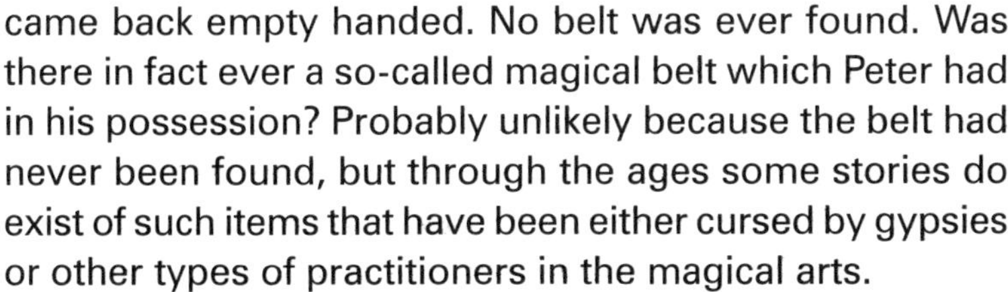

came back empty handed. No belt was ever found. Was there in fact ever a so-called magical belt which Peter had in his possession? Probably unlikely because the belt had never been found, but through the ages some stories do exist of such items that have been either cursed by gypsies or other types of practitioners in the magical arts.

During the examination process with Peter's daughter and his mistress (said to be a distant cousin of Peter's), the court came to the conclusions that the two women had a hand in the matter of the slayings; also it was believed to be a sin against God to have relations with the blood line of a family member. The town's people believed the Devil had his hand in this matter and such crimes needed to be taken seriously. On October 31, 1589, all three were put to the death. Peter was to be made an example for these types of monstrous crimes, for they would not be tolerated across the lands. Peter's body, while still alive, was placed onto a large wheel, his flesh was ripped in places by a pair of hot pliers. His arms and legs were to be broken or crushed by the head of a wooden ax. After this had been done, his head was to be removed and the remains of Peter's lifeless body was to be burned into ashes. The court issued that Peter's head be placed along with a handmade wooden wolf upon a long pole going through the very wheel where his body once lay during his execution. The names of his victims were written on the wood for everyone to see. This would make sure to scare anyone else from thinking of committing such crimes again.

While Peter was going though his public execution, behind the scenes the two women were being raped by the guards and other men of sort. After the rapes had been completed the women endured having parts of their bodies' flayed (being skinned alive or parts of the bodies' skin removed) and then burned alive in the public square.

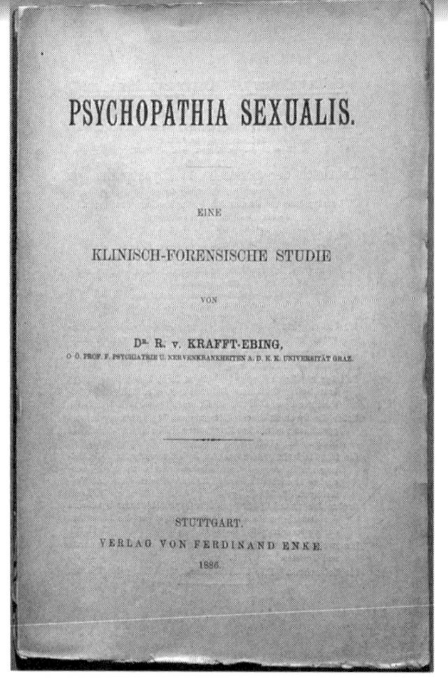
PSYCHOPATHIA SEXUALIS.

EINE

KLINISCH-FORENSISCHE STUDIE

VON

Dr. R. v. KRAFFT-EBING,

O. Ö. PROF. F. PSYCHIATRIE U. NERVENKRANKHEITEN A. D. K. K. UNIVERSITÄT GRAZ.

STUTTGART.

VERLAG VON FERDINAND ENKE.

1886.

Psychopathia Sexualis by Dr. R. v. Krafft-Ebing 1886.

Peter was a psychopathic murderer with a severe case of cannibalism—a taste for human flesh—that ran throughout his blood stream. What a better way to say his crimes were due to being a werewolf, rather then he had an illness or mental disease. Yes, this case of Peter Stubbe is forever stuck in my mind and yet I feel some form of sympathy for how each had died that day, though it is true that their victims were never given a choice to live or die. So its goes back the old saying: "an eye for an eye."

VINCENZ VERZENI

This is sure a story which will either turn your stomach or peak your interest into the earlier type psychopathic murderers.

In a village back in 1872, a naked fourteen-year-old girl was discovered along a small village road, mutilated to death with her insides ripped out, chunks taken out of her thigh that were bitten out. Some of her remains had disappeared from the horrific scene of the crime, and other parts of her body were dispersed all over the ground.

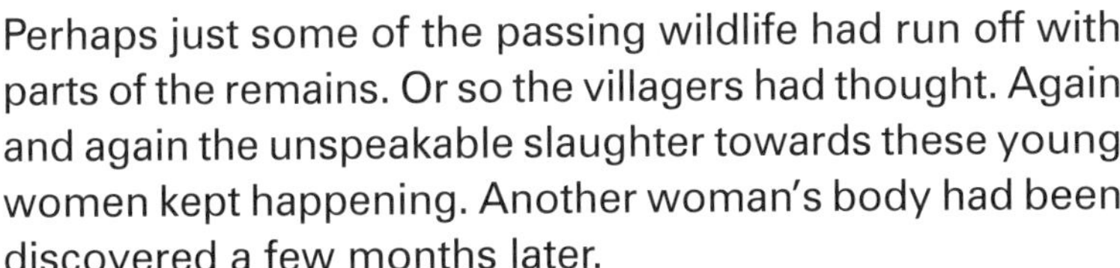

Perhaps just some of the passing wildlife had run off with parts of the remains. Or so the villagers had thought. Again and again the unspeakable slaughter towards these young women kept happening. Another woman's body had been discovered a few months later.

How these women must have suffered, lying on the ground naked with their bodies bitten and torn apart at the abdomen. Fear struck the entire village—until one nineteen-year-old victim was able to get away from the attacker and had given authorities a name. Vincenz Verzeni was the young man's name and he was just twenty-two years old. The suspicions of the authorities and villagers had been right.

Verzeni confessed to being guilty of these terrible sexual mutilations of the young women. It aroused his sexual pleasure placing his hands around their necks; if he got an erection before his victim passed out or died, he would let the woman survive. If not, then he would viciously mutilate the body. Each victim's body was not raped while she was alive, but rather while deceased. Verzeni even confessed that he once drank one of his victim's blood and tore out parts of her remains, which he enjoyed carrying because this action gave him such an extreme sexual sensation.

During Verzeni's questioning by authorities, he spoke:

> I had an unspeakable delight in strangling women, experiencing during the act erections and real sexual pleasure. It was even a pleasure only to smell female clothing. The feeling of pleasure while strangling them was much greater than that which I experienced while masturbating. I took great delight in drinking their blood. It also gave me the greatest pleasure to pull the hair-pins out of the hair of my victims.

Verzeni continues as he states:

> I took the clothing and intestines, because of the pleasure it gave me to smell and touch them. At last my mother came to suspect me, because she noticed spots of semen on my shirt after each murder or attempt at one. I am not crazy, but in the moment of strangling my victims I saw nothing else. After the commission of the deeds I was satisfied and felt well. It never occurred to me to touch or look at the genitals or such things. It satisfied me to seize the women by the neck and suck their blood. To this very day I am ignorant of how a woman is formed. During the strangling and after it, I pressed myself on the entire body without thinking of one part more than another.
>
> I could not find much information as to how exactly Verzeni had died while serving life in a hard labor prison camp, but the medical doctors did evaluate the abnormalities of his body parts; alive or deceased is something of a mystery due to lack of public historical records of this case. Results of the examination came up with a few facts that Verzeni's skull and cranium was larger than normal healthy individuals, one ear seemed larger than the other and some deformities could be seen within both ears. Also, during the medical evaluation of the body; doctors discovered that Verzeni's penis was abnormally large in size.

Now a wonderful German sexologist/psychiatrist by the name of Richard von Krafft-Ebing wrote a book based on case studies in 1886 called *Psychopathia Sexualis*; one of those cases was on covering Verzeni. Within this book Dr. von Krafft-Ebing writes about individuals with a bestial appetite towards their victims, forms of Sadism, the mental state of the murderers during sexual crimes, homosexuality, and sexual fetishism. During Dr. von Krafft-Ebing's earlier works, he published a controversial book which covered different areas of mental illness. One of the things he pondered upon was whether or not bestial sexuality and murder could have had hereditary factors. This book was called *Textbook of Insanity* written in 1879. During Dr. von Krafft-Ebing's career, he pushed for the use of different types of therapy to treat patients rather than just imprisonment.

A writer/director by the name of Bret Wood actually made a movie with his own twists and plots based on several of the cases and stories from the original book *Psychopathia Sexualis*. The movie, which came out in 2006, shares the exact name. If you have an interest in learning more about this movie and Bret Woods, I suggest checking out his website at www.bretwood.blogspot.com.

LUDWIG TESSNOW

During my research on the Ludwig Tessnow case which happened during 1901, I came across a great article in German called *"Das Blut der Opfer"* or in English, *"The blood of the victims,"* which was written by Ulrich Zander. Here are some very interesting facts written about the case.

On the evening of July the 1st, the two five and seven year old sons of wagon maker Grabbert from the seaside resort of Gohren went missing. A hastily arranged crew tried to find the children in the early morning hours the following day. Eventually, when they found the corpses, they were mutilated, the heads and limbs separated and internal organs scattered up to 400 meters away. The bodies were also partially skinned and pieces of the corpses were found even days later. Near the area of the corpses, a large fist-sized rock was found with a blood smear congruent to the killing wounds found on the victims.

Tessnow works near Gohrener in a neighboring place called Baabe, and was observed by several witnesses in the proximity of the scene. When approached about the killings and asked about blood stained clothes that were found, Tessnow explained to authorities that the "bloodstains" were not blood at all but merely paint! Tessnow worked as a carpenter and house painter using his occupation as his alibi. He seemed a very staid character, showing no obvious signs of mental illness.

So, basically, the above paragraph is stating that Ludwig lied his way out of an arrest from the local authorities. By stating that the stains on his shirt were only due to being a carpenter and could be some form of paint. What could the authorities actually do, for no proof was shown for the arrest of Lugwig? A few years prior, Lugwig was also under suspicion for another double murder (in September of 1898) of two young girls. The crimes were committed almost exactly in the same way as the 1901 murders.

Not soon after the murders in Göhren, a man named Paul Uhlenhuth, who was a biologist, had discovered a scientific medical method for investigations and identification of human blood.

Now Ulrich Zander goes on to write:

> Its Uhlenhuth, which on Hygieneinstitut of the university Greifswald worked and had been active as an assistant of the world-famous physician Robert Cook before, published results on 7 February 1901 in the *German Medical Weekly Revue* in the essay "a method for the distinction of the different kinds of blood, in the special for the differential-diagnostic proof of the people blood." It had found out that rabbits, to which one injected cow's milk in the aqueous part of their blood, for which blood serums formed, repelling off against the strange protein. If one mixes then the serum with cow's milk, a cloudy, flockiger precipitation results from these defense materials. The milk protein "is precipitated." Because of, speak depressing effect marked the researcher the defense materials "fällenden" as "Präzipitine." In addition Uhlenhuth recognized that rabbit rum, which had formed by injection of chicken blood fällte also the

 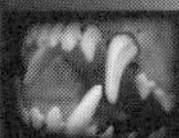

> protein in the chicken blood." "Uhlenhuth had however further-vigorous still for weeks, until he won a rabbit rum, which reacted only to people blood. Thus it had become possible to assign blood marks, all the same whether age-old or fresh to identify not only as blood but also to the appropriate animal species – or humans.

On June 12th some sheep had been brutally slaughtered with their body parts dispersed all over the ground. The owner of the sheep was at the town's pub having a few drinks, so authorities knew the owner had an alibi. Again, Ludwig was questioned because he'd been spotted at that same location. Yet again, authorities heard that the stains on his shirt were from his work as a carpenter.

But this time it was all over for Ludwig. While he was running at the mouth with excuses, his blood was being tested and identified by Uhlenhuth. Needless to say, Tessnow was arrested, and convicted of the crimes. He was executed by beheading at the Greifswald prison in 1904.

JACK OWEN SPILLMAN III

The media has dubbed Jack Spillman "The Werewolf Butcher." Personally, I would not go to the extreme of calling him a werewolf, but I can see where they would get that idea. He was violent, bloody, and severely mentally unstable. Due to my history as a corrections officer at the State Prison here in New Hampshire, many people feel compelled to discuss serial murderers and rapists with me. Most often they want to hear the gritty details of the people I saw on a routine basis, people much like those in this chapter. The actual fact is that working day-to-day, I became immune (like most officers) to the inmates' crimes. I focused solely on doing my job and keeping them out of society until they *maxed out*, meaning that the inmate had served their time.

However, being around these individuals everyday from eight to sixteen hours, you learn a few things. Individuals like Jack Spillman got their jollies by stalking, watching, and waiting for that "right" moment—that was where the thrill was. The actual killing was like a reward for their patience; they love the silence after a struggle.

Jack Spillman's hunting grounds were in Washington State; the first known killing took place in East Wenatchee. During 1995, authorities discovered the bodies of a mother and daughter; it was clear from the beginning that this was no rash impulsive murder, but something well planned out. There were no signs of forced entry; the mutilated bodies of Rita (the mother) and her 15-year-old daughter, Mandy, had been carefully arranged, the private parts of both women had been removed and placed either next to, or on, the other victim.

Local authorities decided to check the recent police logs to see if anything would catch their eye; in fact, something did. Around 2am that morning, an individual had been arrested on the suspicion of burglary, but what was important was the location of the arrest. It had been not too far from the crime committed hours prior. Without any solid proof that the suspect, Jack Owen, brutally murdered the two females, authorities had to release him. Meanwhile, a search of the area had been done; a knife which still had remnants of blood on the blade was tested with the victim's blood at the crime scene. It was a match with one of the victims. Doing a little more research into Jack's police record was quite revealing. The authorities discovered that he had previously been charged with rape, burglary, and attempted rape. There were also statements in the file pertinent to a mother and child who had been rooming with Jack. The child had disappeared and had never been found. Unfortunately, nothing within the file gave police evidence without a doubt of Jack's guilt. Although he had been arrested for rape and attempted rape, nothing in his file showed this type of vile behavior. Still the authorities believed they had the killer.

Under tight surveillance, authorities caught Jack trying to dispose of a blood-stained ski mask. After the test came back which matched the ski mask and victims blood samples, the arrest was then finally made. The mask had blood stains around the mouth's opening, which lead to the conclusion that some of the victim's blood was drunk. While searching the residence of Jack's home and vehicle, more hair particles and blood evidence was found.

If you want to learn more about Jack Spillman, I suggest checking out *Sex Related Homicides and Death Investigation* by Vernon Gebreth. In an article written by Katherine Ramsland called "The Werewolf Syndrome: Compulsive Bestial Slaughters," she speaks about Jack Spillman. Katherine used Geberth for her research and it really helped to give a little insight into the mentality of this killer:

> Geberth indicates that Spillman's cellmate told authorities that he had "bragged that his ambition was to be the most famous serial murderer in the country." He thought of himself as a werewolf, he said, and thus stalked "prey" the way a ravenous beast might do. He had studied other killers to learn how to avoid being caught,

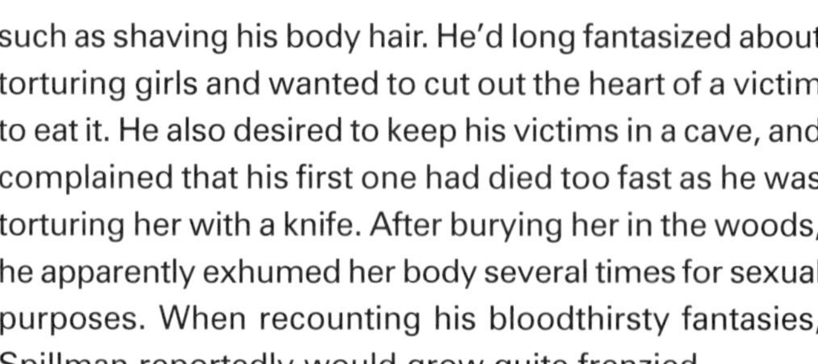

> such as shaving his body hair. He'd long fantasized about torturing girls and wanted to cut out the heart of a victim to eat it. He also desired to keep his victims in a cave, and complained that his first one had died too fast as he was torturing her with a knife. After burying her in the woods, he apparently exhumed her body several times for sexual purposes. When recounting his bloodthirsty fantasies, Spillman reportedly would grow quite frenzied.

Jack Owen pleaded guilty during his trial in 1996 to three counts of aggravated murder (one of which was a 9-year-old girl in 1994) to avoid the death penalty. He was sentenced to life in prison without any chance of parole.

THE MODERN THERIANTHROPE

I am placing this chapter under Mysteries, simply because it is a mystery. What causes one to knowingly become a werewolf, or to acknowledge their wolf-like tendencies? In high schools today, there are wolf packs forming; yes, you heard me...wolf packs. High school guidance counselors feel that their need to be a pack is like any other clique in high school—they are searching for individuality, a way to express themselves and create an identity while at the same time, finding a safe place to belong.

High school is not the only place you will find the modern therianthrope, although I have found that they are the most common. A lot of what I researched hearkened back more towards shamanism than anything that modern movies could create. A therian feels spiritually that they are not all human, and have a strong connection or kinship to another species; this can be wolf, rat, cat, or any other

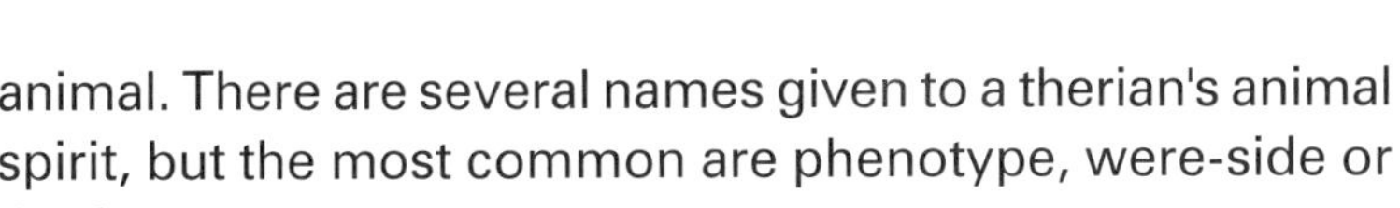

animal. There are several names given to a therian's animal spirit, but the most common are phenotype, were-side or theriotype.

If you think of the Nagual, which we spoke of in earlier chapters, or the totem animals depicted in Native American beliefs, it is not difficult to see how we in our modern culture could still feel that kinship with animals. These modern shapeshifters look at the animal as a part of them, a piece of them, and much like someone being born with blue eyes, they say there is not a choice. It simply is something they were born with. Most therianthropes eventually find their middle ground and become wonderful members of society, but much like growing from child to adult, it takes time and learning.

The therian community believes that they can transform during a process called shifting. There are several different ways they do this, including physical shifting, which from my research has more to do with the eyes than growing hair all over the body and giant fangs. This is something that most therians will do willingly, usually when they are alone at home, or with others like them when they can be their true selves. There are different grades or types of shifting, here is a brief explanation of the shifts:

ASTRAL SHIFT

Astral projection is the spiritual means of detaching your spirit from your body, allowing your spirit to travel in what many people call the astral plane. There is no danger in doing this as there will always be a connection between spirit and body. The astral plane is much like a lucid dream; it is very real. The way to go into the astral plane is through meditation. In the astral, therians can truly be themselves in their full form. If you use the visualization from the mental shift (as described below) substitute the part of the meditation where your creature walks into you with you turning into the creature.

DREAM SHIFT

A moment of lucid dreaming, where you are able to truly become your phenotype. Most otherkin really crave those moments when in dream they are their animal in body and spirit. It feels like home to them, whereas on this earthly plane, they many feel trapped in their skin.

MENTAL SHIFT

The most common kind of shift that takes place, it is the change from a logical human mind into one that is more primitive or animalistic. This can happen on command or anytime during waking hours. Supposedly, it can be triggered if the therian is in a state of extreme stress. Most therians (especially in the beginning) will find difficulty in a voluntary shift to their animal counterpart, but there are meditations you can use to help you through the process. Here is one:

> Visualize yourself in an environment that mimics that of your animal (i.e., woods for wolves, arctic for polar bears, bamboo forests for pandas) see your animal spirit walk towards you. Visualize it approaching you and sitting down in front of you. As it sits there it becomes translucent, like a ghost. Slowly it moves forward and walks into your body. You can feel the power surge through you from this animal spirit and as you look around, you begin to see things as this animal would (i.e., if it's color blind, you are as well). You move your arm and realize you no longer feel fingers but paws or hooves...you slowly make the change.

Carry this visualization through several times a week so that you brain can adapt to calling forth your animal self. These types of shifts do not cause your personality to become aggressive or for you to lose control of your human mind; it merely helps your conscious self to take a backseat.

PHANTOM SHIFT

When an amputee loses a limb, oftentimes, they can still feel as if it were there. A phantom shift works the same, if the person's phenotype is a wolf, then they will feel that they have a tail. The most common phantom shifts are fur, ears and tails. These shifts are invisible to the naked eye but, to a therian it is very, very real.

PHYSICAL SHIFT

Highly debated amongst the otherkin community, physical shifting is the belief that one can actually change into their phenotype, much like in the movies! In my research, I have come across many therians who believe that they can make this shift at will, but as of yet, I have seen no evidence to prove their claim.

The most common physical shift is that of the eyes—color changes in particular. Sometimes it even feels uncomfortable standing in an upright position, their legs will not work properly when standing. The only position they feel comfort in is the one their phenotype would normally take. Most therians believe that p-shifting is not possible and the scientific community credits the eye color change to a manipulation of the portion of the brain which controls the lipids in the eyes and that these effects are short lived.

SPIRITUAL SHIFT

Think of how Buddha remembered all of his past lives, now imagine what it would have been like had one of his past-life selves took control. That is similar to what happens to otherkin when they have a spiritual shift. Their animal self from a past life, steps forward. This can be extremely like a mental shift but is nowhere near the same. These past-life experiences can actually cause feelings of anxiety, stress, or fear; they can also go the exact opposite and feel strong, stable, and empowered. It all depends on how the shifter felt prior to their passing. This can be accompanied by memories that the animal had throughout its life. Much like a mental shift, these can happen at random.

Most people believe that therianthropy is a psychological condition, one that most therians are actually aware of! However, therians also claim that they differ from clinical lycanthropy in many ways. Most therians are non-violent and take comfort in their animal type. These modern were-people display a variety of different characteristics. I have found these similarities through speaking with different therians:

- Awkward social skills
- Above average creative visualization skills
- Highly intelligent
- Feeling of being alone or on the outside of society
- Do not trust authority (and in some cases outright disrespect it)
- Anxiety
- Bouts of depression

These are just to name a few; that is not to say that every therian is dark and broody, because I have met more than a few happy-go-lucky types. I believe that the therian community, much like any other, has a diverse range of personalities, perspectives, and ideas regarding their spiritual beliefs.

Overall, our modern day werewolves, were-cats and were-penguins (yes, I said it!) are fun loving, upstanding members of society just trying to figure out how to make it all work!

CONCLUSION

The question that still burns within the mind of this writer is: Does the werewolf really lurk in the darkness or is it just our way of expressing our darkest animalistic urges?

One could write a thousand-page text and still only touch a tenth of the werewolf mythos, magick, and mentality. There is so much to cover regarding this beast in all facets of our society, whether you take a literal, theological, or psychological approach. The werewolf will always be shrouded in mystery, whether it once existed, or only existed in our minds, and spirits.

The research that took place during the writing of this book only confirmed in my mind that the threat of some great hairy violent beast is the least of our worries; it is those clothed in human skin which howls at the moon who we need to fear.

I have brought forth to you, the reader, the myth, mysteries, and magic of the werewolf. Whether you believe in the creature or not, I hope that this book helped to shed light on who or what the werewolf could be.

BE SAFE,
KATIE BOYD

APPENDIX

"Never moon a werewolf."

~Mike Binder

A LIST OF NOTORIOUS SHAPESHIFTERS

BERSERKERS

Norse warriors who were thought to use their rage to shapeshift into bears and wolves.

BOUDA

A matriarchal African tribe, thought to be capable of changing into were-hyenas. Other were-hyenas, known as Qora, were punished in the old Kingdom of Kaffa, now part of Ethiopia.

ENCANTADOS

According to stories from Brazil, they are "the enchanted ones," creatures from an underwater realm, usually dolphins with the ability to change into humans.

THE FROG PRINCE

A transformed prince who must be restored to his original form; few variants specify why he was transformed.

THE FROG PRINCESS

A fairy tale of a frog married to a prince, concludes with her transformation into a beautiful princess. In some variants, she was originally a princess.

JAPANESE FOXES (KITSUNE)

In Japanese myth, foxes would fool unsuspecting humans by assuming other forms, most often, beautiful women. Similar fox myths abound from other countries such as China, Korea, Vietnam, and even the United States.

LESZI

Spirits of Slavic mythology, capable of changing into any creature or plant.

LOATHLY LADY

A lady transformed into a hideous shape. Upon her marriage to a knight, the spell is sufficiently broken that she could appear lovely at night, or during the day, and she informs the knight that he has to select which one. When he asks which *she* prefers, the spell is entirely broken, and she remains lovely day and night.

LOKI

Trickster god of the Norse pantheon.

THE MASTER MAID

She hails from the fairy tale of the same name and can transform objects to block the pursuit by her troll masters—a common trait of women rescued from evil magicians or monsters.

NAHUALES

In Mexican and Mesoamerican lore, shamans that have shapeshifting abilities, usually turning into coyotes, wolves or jaguars.

NAGAS

Snake-people of Asian countries, especially India & Nepal; may appear either as transforming between human and snake, or as a cross between the two (such as the upper torso being human and the lower torso being serpentine); some Nagas may also assume the form of dragons.

ODIN

War/death god of the Norse pantheon, often changes forms becoming men, women, children, and other forms.

PROTEUS

A Greek sea god who was capable of changing his form to avoid being captured.

PÚCA

This and some other Celtic spirits and Síde (fairies) can change their form at will and typically pose as animals or loved ones. Leprechauns turn into hideous creatures to scare you into releasing them when captured.

RUNA-UTURUNGU

Were-jaguars from Argentina (regional name); also spelled runa-uturuncu.

SELKIE

Seal-maidens and seal-men of Irish/Scottish myth.

SPRIGGAN

Cat-like fae.

SWAN MAIDEN

Shapeshifting birds from worldwide mythology.

TANUKI

Japanese raccoon dogs that have a strong mythological background as shapechangers who are adept at mimicking inanimate objects.

TENGU

Japanese bird monsters who can shapeshift to human form.

THUNDERBIRDS

Huge birdlike creatures described in the lore of several Native American tribes; some thunderbirds turn into human beings.

CHILD BALLAD # 44, "THE TWO MAGICIANS"

The two magicians of Child Ballad #44, "The Two Magicians" stage their respective attempts to escape and capture as a series of transformations into shapes that can flee or hide, and chase or work into the hiding place. This is a common motif in pursuit in fairy tales.

VAMPIRES
Corpses who can turn into wolves and/or bats.

WOLFWERES
Wolves who can become human or semi-human.

WENDIGO
A shapeshifter from Canadian legend said to transform only after the individual fated to transform has for some reason succumbed to or been forced into the practice of human cannibalism.

WERE-CATS
Feline shapeshifters.

WEREWOLVES
Humans who turn into wolves.

PTESANWI
A woman of Lakota legend, rumored to have appeared as a white buffalo. There are numerous tales of shapeshifting in Native American mythology, the most notable being prey animals such as buffalo and deer, and predators such as bears and wolves.

YAGUARETÉ-ABÁ
Were-jaguars from Argentina and Bolivia (regional name), also uturunco.

ZMEI
Romanian mythological creatures, similar to Ogres.

ZEUS
Head of the Greek pantheon, who routinely transformed into various animal forms and had sexual congress with human women to beget half-god mortals.

RESOURCES

Here are some wonderful websites which you may gain more knowledge on the subjects which I've covered and some great ones to just check out!

KATIE BOYD'S WEBSITES:
www.katieboyd.net
www.ghostquest.org
TenacityRadio.com

DON SMITH WEBSITES:
http://donsmith74.wordpress.com
InvestComics.com

WEREWOLF SITES:
www.monstrous.com
www.werewolves.com
www.werewolfpage.com

COMIC BOOK SITES:
www.baneofthewerewolf.com
www.bluewaterprod.com
www.marvel.com
www.whoissaintjames.com

MEDICAL SITES:
www.cdc.gov
www.genome.gov
www.mayoclinic.com
www.nccn.net/~wwithin/abortedtissue.htm
www.nimh.nih.gov
www.wormsandgermsblog.com

OTHER GREAT SITES:

www.bloody-discusting.com
www.ghostwalklive.com
www.knightparanormal.com
www.planetparanormal.com
www.practicalhomicide.com
www.sideshowworld.com
www.skepticworld.com
www.spiritsofnewengland.org
www.trutv.com

MORE ABOUT KATIE'S BOOKS

What people are saying about:
DEVILS AND DEMONOLOGY IN THE 21ST CENTURY

"This book is a FANTASTIC debunking tool for teams who may face this dilemma someday or as a guide if you are learning about the science and want to delve into the history of where it all started, how and when."

~Shannon Sylvia
(Formerly of *Ghost Hunters International*)

"It's hard to teach an old witch new tricks, but Katie Boyd is a master of her craft and taught me quite a bit. For example, her chapter on Negative Thoughtforms is a MUST for anyone working in the paranormal realm."

~Marla Brooks
Host of *Stirring The Cauldron*
Author, *Workplace Spells*

"Devils and Demonology in the 21st Century is a thorough accounting of the history and lore of demonology in the world today and throughout history. Katie Boyd has written an excellent resource guide detailing demonology in the world's religions and gives a concise accounting of demonic names, habits and habitats. This is a great book for anyone who has an interest in the dark forces at work in the world today. Katie also gives you the benefit

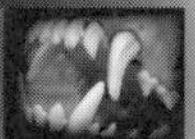

of her years of research, knowledge and experience in how to deal with these forces should you come in contact with them during an investigation or in your daily life. You will find this a fascinating read that is hard to put down. Devils and Demonology in the 21st Century is a must-have book for any person studying demonology, the world's religions or just the curious reader."

~Bob Davis
CEO Planet Paranormal Broadcast *Network*
www.PlanetParanormal.com

"*Devils & Demonology in the 21st Century* is THE most comprehensive book released in recent years on the subject of Demonology. Covering everything from the history and beginnings of this unique and very misunderstood field of paranormal work, through Occultism, working with seals and sigils, identifying the difference between demonic possession and psychology and much, much more, it is a truly definitive work. In the last section of the book, Katie Boyd has included what I feel is the best field guide on this subject that I have ever seen. I learned more from this one book on the subject of demonology, negative thoughtforms, demons and how to protect yourself when investigating then I have learned from any other book on the this subject. This is a MUST read for any paranormal investigator. It also is a fantastic field reference and I take it along on every investigation our team does, as it has come in very handy on more than one occasion. If you only own one book on the subject of demonology, then this is the one to have!"

~Jack Kenna
Paranormal Investigator for SPIRITS of New England

"If you are interested in the paranormal at all, this book is a must read! It includes a generous sampling of all topics from early occultism to Ouija boards and examples of real cases. We actually use this book when training new team members or dealing with unique activity during investigations!"

~Tom Watkins
Knight Paranormal

BIBLIOGRAPHY

Andrade, Manuel J. "Quileute Texts." *Columbia University Contributions to Anthropology* 12 (2). New York. 1931.

Baring-Gould, Sabine. *The Book of Werewolves*. New York: Causeway Books. 1973. p. 8.

Baring-Gould Sabine, *The Book of Werewolves: Being an Account of a Terrible Superstition* London: Smith, Elder, and Company, 1865, pp. 124-128.

Barrett, Francis. "The Magus." London, 1801. http://www.imdb.com/title/tt0072431/quotes.

Bathgate, Michael. *The Fox's Craft in Japanese Religion and Folklore: Transformations, and Duplicities.* New York: Routledge, 2004.

Boas, Franz. *Folk-Tales of Salishan and Sahaptin Tribes — Memoirs of the American Folk-Lore Society*, vol. 11. Lancaster and New York: American Folk-Lore Society, 1917, pp. 53: 198-200.

Bores, George. *"The Damnable Life and Death of one Stubbe Peeter." London Chapbook of 1590.*

Buck, William. *Ramayana*. Berkeley: University of California Press, 1976.

Dowson, John. *A classical dictionary of Hindu mythology and religion, geography, history, and literature*. London: Trübner, 1879.

Elliot Griffis ,William. *Welsh Fairy Tales.* New York: Thomas Y. Crowell Company, 1921, no. 3, pp. 15-20.

Encyclopedia Britannica Online. "Lycaon." Encyclopedia Britannica. 2010. 03 Aug. 2010 <http://www.britannica.com/EBchecked/topic/352501/Lycaon>.

Karl Bartsch, *Sagen. Märchen und Gebräuche aus Meklenburg.* Wien: Wilhelm Braumüller, 1879, v. 1, no. 185, pp. 150-151.

ESSENTIAL WEREWOLF BY NIGHT VOL. 2. New York: Marvel Comics. 2007. p. 5.

Freeman-Mitford, A. B. *Tales of Old Japan*. London: Macmillan, 1871, 1890.

Garlipp P, Godeck-Koch T, Haltenhof H, Dietrich DE. "Lycanthropy, zooanthropism, and discussion of a psychopathological phenomenon." [in German]. *Fortschr Neural Psychiatry*. 2001; 69: 215 – 20.

Geberth, Vernon. *Sex-related Homicides and Death Investigation*. CRC Press, 2005.

GRIFFITH, M. A., RALPH T. H. *THE RÁMÁYAN OF VÁLMÍKI* London: Trübner & Co. Benares: E. J. Lazarus and Co. 1870-1874.

Hamel, Frank. *Human Animals: Werewolves & Other Transformations.* New Hyde Park, N.Y.: University Books, 1969. (pp. 88-102).

Hearn, Lafcadio. Kwaidan: *Stories and Studies of Strange Things.* Boston, Houghton, Mifflin and Co. 1904.

Herodotus. Trans. George Rawlinson. "History of Herodotus" 440 B.C.E. Publisher/dates unknown.

Keck PE, Pope HG, Hudson JI, McElroy SL, Kuilick AR. "Lycanthropy: alive and well in the twentieth century." *Psychol Med.* 1988; pp113 – 20.

Kershaw, N ed. trans. "Battle of Hafsfjord" Anglo-Saxon and Norse Poems, University Press; Cambridge: 1922. pp. 88-91.

O'Donnell, Elliot. *WEREWOLVES*. London; Methuen and Co. LTD, 1912: pp 56-60.

Ovid. " Metamorphoses." 1 A.C.E.: Book 1.

Mackay, Charles. *Extraordinary Popular Delusions & the Madness of Crowds*. New York: Crown Trade Paperbacks. 1980.

Moghaddas, Ali-Reza MD and Mitra Nasseri MD. Archives of Iranian Medicine, Volume 7, Number 2, 2004: 130 – 132.

Narayan, R. K. The Ramayana. New York: Penguin, 1972.

Pausanias. Description of Greece. Translated by Jones, W. H. S. and Omerod, H. A. Loeb Classical Library Volumes. Cambridge, MA, Harvard University Press; London, William Heinemann Ltd. 1918.

Rig Veda, tr. Ralph T.H. Griffith, Publisher unknown. 1896.

Ramsland, Katherine. "The Werewolf Syndrome: Compulsive Bestial Slaughters." TruTV Crime Library. 3 June 2010. <http://www.trutv.com/library/crime/criminal_mind/psychology/werewolf_killers/3.html>.

Sidky, H. *Witchcraft, Lycanthropy, Drugs, and Disease: An Anthropological Study of the European Witch-Hunts*. New York: Peter Lang Publishing, Inc. 1997.

Thompson, David. *Japanese Fairy Tale Series Vol 1. Num. 5.* Tokyo, T. Hasegawa: 1885.

Wratislaw, A.H. *Sixty Folk-Tales from Exclusively Slavonic Sources.* London: Elliot Stock, 1889, pp. 290-291.

Zander, Ulrich. *"Das Blut der Opfer"* Berliner Morgenpost 10 June 2008. 6 June 2010. <"http://www.morgenpost.de/incoming/article231398/Das_Blut_der_Opfer.html">